30
Essential
Lessons
from the
Life of
Christ

Table of Contents

30
Essential
Lessons
from the
Life of
Christ

Freeman-Smith, a division of Worthy Media, Inc.
134 Franklin Road, Suite 200, Brentwood, Tennessee 37027

The quoted ideas expressed in this book (but not Scripture verses) are not, in all cases, exact quotations, as some have been edited for clarity and brevity. In all cases, the author has attempted to maintain the speaker's original intent. In some cases, quoted material for this book was obtained from secondary sources, primarily print media. While every effort was made to ensure the accuracy of these sources, the accuracy cannot be guaranteed. For additions, deletions, corrections, or clarifications in future editions of this text, please write Freeman-Smith.

Scripture quotations are taken from:

The Holy Bible, King James Version

The Holy Bible, New International Version (NIV) Copyright © 1973, 1978, 1984, by International Bible Society. Used by permission of Zondervan Publishing House. All rights reserved.

The Holy Bible, New King James Version (NKJV) Copyright © 1982 by Thomas Nelson, Inc. Used by permission.

The New American Standard Bible®, (NASB) Copyright © 1960, 1962, 1963, 1968, 1971, 1972, 1973, 1975, 1977, 1995 by The Lockman Foundation. Used by permission.

The Message (MSG)- This edition issued by contractual arrangement with NavPress, a division of The Navigators, U.S.A. Originally published by NavPress in English as THE MESSAGE: The Bible in Contemporary Language copyright 2002-2003 by Eugene Peterson. All rights reserved.

The Holman Christian Standard Bible™ (HCSB) Copyright © 1999, 2000, 2001 by Holman Bible Publishers. Used by permission.

Cover Design by Kim Russell / Wahoo Designs
Page Layout by Bart Dawson

ISBN 978-1-60587-344-2

Printed in the United States of America

What do you think of Jesus

Do you have a personal acquaintance with him

What role does Jesus play in my life

Introduction

If you're like most people, you simply can't remember the first time you heard the name Jesus—His name, like His Good News, is likely to be woven into the fabric of your life. But perhaps you haven't thought as much about the lessons that you can learn from the life and the words of Jesus. If so, this book can help.

This text examines 30 lessons from the life and the teachings of Jesus. That means that for the next month, you'll have 30 different opportunities to consider the role that Christ plays in your life today, and the role that you intend for Him to play tomorrow.

Hannah Whitall Smith correctly observed, "The crucial question for each of us is this: What do you think of Jesus, and do you yet have a personal acquaintance with Him?" How do you answer that question? Do you have a personal acquaintance with the carpenter from Galilee, and are you a different person because of that relationship? During the next 30 days, you'll be asked to think carefully about your answer.

As you read this text, take time to consider the role that Jesus plays in your life—and, more importantly, the role that He should play. Be mindful of Christ's lessons, and apply them. When you do, you'll be blessed today, tomorrow, and forever.

A Timeline of the Life of Jesus

(Dates Are Approximate)

6/5 BC: Jesus is born in Bethlehem.

6/5 BC: Jesus is presented in the temple at Jerusalem.

6/5 BC: Mary and Joseph escape with the baby Jesus to Egypt.

6/5 BC: Mary and Joseph return to Nazareth with the baby Jesus.

7/8 AD: A young Jesus goes to the temple in Jerusalem.

26 AD: Jesus is baptized by John in the Jordan River.

26 AD: In the wilderness, Jesus is tempted by Satan.

26 AD: Jesus performs His first miracle at Cana by turning water into wine.

27 AD: Jesus removes money changers from the temple.

27 AD: Jesus heals the sick and performs other miracles.

27-28 AD: Jesus gains followers and chooses 12 disciples.

28 AD: Jesus preaches the Sermon on the Mount at Capernaum.

28 AD: Jesus travels through Galilee teaching and performing miracles.

28 AD: Jesus sends His disciples to preach and heal.

28 AD: John the Baptist is killed by Herod.

29 AD: Jesus feeds the 5,000, walks on water, and performs other miracles.

29 AD: Jesus tells His disciples He will die soon.

29 AD: Jesus visits Mary and Martha; He raises Lazarus from the dead.

30 AD: Jesus makes His triumphal return to Jerusalem.

30 AD: The Last Supper.

30 AD: Jesus is crucified and buried on a Friday. On Sunday, He rises from the dead and appears to His followers. Forty days later, He ascends to heaven.

Source: Biblenet.net

Lesson 1

Christ Offers Eternal Life

Jesus said to her, "I am the resurrection and the life.
The one who believes in Me, even if he dies,
will live. Everyone who lives and believes in Me
will never die—ever. Do you believe this?"

John 11:25-26 HCSB

THE LESSON

Jesus makes an amazing promise: those who believe in Him
will receive the priceless gift of eternal life.

How marvelous it is that God became a man and walked among us! Had He not chosen to do so, we might feel removed from a distant Creator. But ours is not a distant God. Ours is a God who understands—far better than we ever could—the essence of what it means to be human.

God understands our hopes, our fears, and our temptations. He understands what it means to be angry and what it costs to forgive. He knows the heart, the conscience, and the soul of every person who has ever lived, including you. And God has a plan of salvation that is intended for you. Accept it. Accept God's gift through the person of His Son Christ Jesus, and then rest assured: God walked among us so that you might have eternal life; amazing though it may seem, He did it for you.

> Salvation consists wholly in being saved from ourselves, or that which we are by nature.
>
> —
>
> *Andrew Murray*

As mere mortals, our vision for the future, like our lives here on earth, is limited. God's vision is not burdened by such limitations: His plans extend throughout all eternity. Thus, God's plans for you are not limited to the ups and downs of everyday life. Your Heavenly Father has bigger things in mind . . . much bigger things.

Let us praise the Creator for His priceless gift, and let us share the Good News with all who cross our paths. We return our Father's love by accepting His grace and by sharing His message and His love. When we do, we are blessed here on earth and throughout all eternity.

Hebrews 5 7-9

As you struggle with the inevitable hardships and occasional disappointments of life, remember that God has invited you to accept His abundance not only for today but also for all eternity. So keep things in perspective. Although you will inevitably encounter occasional defeats in this world, you'll have all eternity to celebrate the ultimate victory in the next.

Gods plan for you is to be saved

Does it stop once you are saved

No!

SOMETHING TO THINK ABOUT

If you have already welcomed Christ into your heart as your personal Savior, then you are safe. If you're still sitting on the fence, the time to accept Him is this very moment.

Focusing on God not our problem fpet plees.

MORE IDEAS ABOUT
SALVATION

And we have seen and we testify that the Father has sent the Son as Savior of the world.

1 John 4:14 HCSB

Blessed be the God and Father of our Lord Jesus Christ, who according to His abundant mercy has begotten us again to a living hope through the resurrection of Jesus Christ from the dead . . . .

1 Peter 1:3 NKJV

This saying is trustworthy and deserving of full acceptance: "Christ Jesus came into the world to save sinners."

1 Timothy 1:15 HCSB

Therefore, if anyone is in Christ, he is a new creation; old things have passed away; behold, all things have become new.

2 Corinthians 5:17 NKJV

Then he escorted them out and said, "Sirs, what must I do to be saved?" So they said, "Believe on the Lord Jesus, and you will be saved—you and your household."

Acts 16:30-31 HCSB

Personal salvation is not an occasional rendezvous with Deity; it is an actual dwelling with God.

Billy Graham

God's goal is not to make you happy. It is to make you his.

Max Lucado

Our salvation comes to us so easily because it cost God so much.

Oswald Chambers

Today is the day of salvation. Some people miss heaven by only eighteen inches—the distance between their heads and their hearts.

Corrie ten Boom

I have been all over the world, and I have never met anyone who regretted giving his or her life to Christ.

Billy Graham

God did everything necessary to provide for our forgiveness by sacrificing His perfect, holy Son as the atoning substitute for our sins.

Franklin Graham

MY THOUGHTS ON . . .
God's promise of eternal life and the nature of
my personal relationship with Jesus.

_____

_____

_____

_____

_____

_____

A PRAYER

Dear Lord, You sent Your Son as the Savior of our world.
Jesus is my Savior, Lord, and my strength. I will share
His Good News with all who cross my path, and I will share
His love with all who need His healing touch.

Amen

Lesson 2

God's Love Is Your Security

May Your faithful love comfort me,
as You promised Your servant.

Psalm 119:76 HCSB

THE LESSON

God's children are secure because He loves them, because He is near to them, and because He has all the resources they need for happiness and fulfillment.

God loves us, and He gives us strength. When every earthly support system fails, God remains steadfast, and His love remains unchanged. When we encounter life's inevitable disappointments and setbacks, God remains faithful. When we suffer losses that leave us breathless, God is always with us, always ready to respond to our prayers, always working in us and through us to turn tragedy into triumph.

God's love for you is bigger and better than you can imagine. In fact, God's love is far too big to comprehend (in this lifetime). But this much we know: God loves you so much that He sent His Son Jesus to come to this earth and to die for you. And, if you've allowed Jesus to reign over your life and your heart, you have already received a gift that is more precious than gold: The gift of eternal life.

> There was no other way for sin's penalty to be paid and for us to be redeemed. The Cross is the measure of God's love.
>
> —
>
> *Billy Graham*

The words of Romans 8 make this promise: "For I am persuaded that neither death nor life, nor angels nor principalities nor powers, nor things present nor things to come, nor height nor depth, nor any other created thing, shall be able to separate us from the love of God which is in Christ Jesus our Lord" (vv. 38-39 NKJV).

Sometimes, in the crush of your daily duties, God may seem far away, but He is not. God is everywhere you have ever been and everywhere you will ever go. He is with you night and day; He knows your thoughts and He hears your prayers. When you earnestly seek Him, you will find Him because He is here, waiting patiently for you to reach out to Him.

Reach out to God today and always. Encourage your family members to do likewise. And then, arm-in-arm with your loved ones, praise God for blessings that are simply too numerous to count.

SOMETHING TO THINK ABOUT

When all else fails, God's love does not. You can always depend upon God's love . . . and He is always your ultimate protection.

MORE IDEAS ABOUT
GOD'S LOVE

God is love, and the one who remains in love remains in God, and God remains in him.

1 John 4:16 HCSB

As the Father loved Me, I also have loved you; abide in My love.

John 15:9 NKJV

[Because of] the Lord's faithful love we do not perish, for His mercies never end. They are new every morning; great is Your faithfulness!

Lamentations 3:22-23 HCSB

For the Lord is good, and His love is eternal; His faithfulness endures through all generations.

Psalm 100:5 HCSB

For I am persuaded that neither death nor life, nor angels nor rulers, nor things present, nor things to come, nor powers, nor height, nor depth, nor any other created thing will have the power to separate us from the love of God that is in Christ Jesus our Lord!

Romans 8:38-39 HCSB

The fact is, God no longer deals with us in judgment but in mercy. If people got what they deserved, this old planet would have ripped apart at the seams centuries ago. Praise God that because of His great love "we are not consumed, for his compassions never fail" (Lam. 3:22).

Joni Eareckson Tada

Being loved by Him whose opinion matters most gives us the security to risk loving, too—even loving ourselves.

Gloria Gaither

There is no pit so deep that God's love is not deeper still.

Corrie ten Boom

Even when we cannot see the why and wherefore of God's dealings, we know that there is love in and behind them, so we can rejoice always.

J. I. Packer

God proved his love on the cross. When Christ hung, and bled, and died, it was God saying to the world—I love you.

Billy Graham

There's nothing you can do to get Him to love you and there's nothing you can do to make Him stop.

Charles Stanley

MY THOUGHTS ON . . .
God's love for me and my family and how we should
respond to His love.

_____

_____

_____

_____

_____

_____

A PRAYER

Thank You, Lord, for Your love. Your love is boundless,
infinite, and eternal. Today, let me pause and reflect upon
Your love for me, and let me share that love with all those who
cross my path. And, as an expression of my love for You, Father,
let me share the saving message of Your Son with a world
in desperate need of His peace.
Amen

Lesson 3

Faith Moves Mountains

I assure you: If anyone says to this mountain,
"Be lifted up and thrown into the sea,"
and does not doubt in his heart, but believes
that what he says will happen, it will be done for him.

Mark 11:23 HCSB

THE LESSON

Jesus promises that if you possess genuine, life-changing faith, you can move mountains for God.

The words of Jesus are clear: if you have faith, you can do miraculous things. And that's good because you live in a world where lots of mountains need to be moved.

Are you a mountain mover whose faith is evident for all to see? Or, are you a spiritual shrinking violet? God needs more men and women who are willing to move mountains for His glory and for His kingdom.

Jesus taught His disciples that if they had faith, they could move mountains. You can too. When you place your faith, your trust, indeed your life in the hands of Christ Jesus, you'll be amazed at the marvelous things He can do. So strengthen your faith through praise, through worship, through Bible study, and through prayer. And trust God's plans. With Him, all things are possible, and He stands ready to open a world of possibilities to you . . . if you have faith.

> Relying on God has to begin all over again every day as if nothing had yet been done.
>
> —
>
> *C. S. Lewis*

Concentration camp survivor Corrie ten Boom relied on faith during her long months of imprisonment and torture. Later, despite the fact that four of her family members had died in Nazi death camps, Corrie's faith was unshaken. She wrote, "There is no pit so deep that God's love is not deeper still." Christians take note: Genuine faith in God means faith in all circumstances, happy or sad, joyful or tragic.

If your faith is being tested to the point of breaking, remember that your Savior is near. If you reach out to Him in faith, He will give you peace and strength. Reach out today. If you touch even the smallest fragment of the Master's garment, He will make you whole. And then, with no further ado, let the mountain moving begin.

SOMETHING TO THINK ABOUT

If you don't have faith, you'll never move mountains. But if you do have faith, there's no limit to the things that you and God, working together, can accomplish.

MORE IDEAS ABOUT
FAITH

For whatever is born of God overcomes the world. And this is the victory that has overcome the world—our faith.

1 John 5:4 NKJV

Now without faith it is impossible to please God, for the one who draws near to Him must believe that He exists and rewards those who seek Him.

Hebrews 11:6 HCSB

Be alert, stand firm in the faith, be brave and strong.

1 Corinthians 16:13 HCSB

For we walk by faith, not by sight.

2 Corinthians 5:7 HCSB

Now the just shall live by faith.

Hebrews 10:38 NKJV

There are a lot of things in life that are difficult to understand. Faith allows the soul to go beyond what the eyes can see.

John Maxwell

The popular idea of faith is of a certain obstinate optimism: the hope, tenaciously held in the face of trouble, that the universe is fundamentally friendly and things may get better.

J. I. Packer

I am truly grateful that faith enables me to move past the question of "Why?"

Zig Ziglar

When you enroll in the "school of faith," you never know what may happen next. The life of faith presents challenges that keep you going—and keep you growing!

Warren Wiersbe

Nothing is more disastrous than to study faith, analyze faith, make noble resolves of faith, but never actually to make the leap of faith.

Vance Havner

Grace calls you to get up, throw off your blanket of helplessness, and to move on through life in faith.

Kay Arthur

MY THOUGHTS ON . . .
The mountains I can move if I have faith in God
and faith in myself.

_____

_____

_____

_____

_____

_____

_____

A PRAYER

Dear Lord, in the darkness of uncertainty, give me faith.
In those moments when I am afraid, give me faith.
When I am discouraged or confused, strengthen my faith in You.
You are the Good Shepherd, let me trust in the perfection of
Your plan and in the salvation of Your Son,
this day and every day of my life.
Amen

Lesson 4

Trust God's Will

My Father! If it is possible, let this cup pass from Me.
Yet not as I will, but as You will.

Matthew 26:39 HCSB

THE LESSON

As He contemplated His death, Jesus accepted God's will. We, too, must learn to trust the Father completely and without reservation.

When Jesus confronted the reality of His impending death on the cross, He asked God if this terrible burden could be lifted. But as He faced the possibility of a suffering that was beyond description, Jesus prayed, "Nevertheless not my will, but thine, be done" (Luke 22:42 KJV). As Christians, we too must be willing to accept God's will, even when we do not fully understand the reasons for the hardships that we must endure.

As human beings with limited understanding, we can never fully understand the will of God. But as believers in a benevolent God, we must always trust the will of our Heavenly Father. When we trust God, we should trust Him without reservation. We should steel ourselves against the inevitable disappointments of today, secure in the knowledge that our Heavenly Father has a plan for the future that only He can see.

> Faith will not always get for us what we want, but it will get what God wants us to have.
>
> —
>
> *Vance Havner*

Grief and suffering visit all of us who live long and love deeply. When we lose a loved one, or when we experience any other profound loss, darkness overwhelms us for a while, and it seems as if we cannot summon the strength to face another day—but, with God's help, we can.

When we confront circumstances that trouble us to the very core of our souls, we must trust God. When we are worried, we must turn our concerns over to Him. When we are anxious, we must be still and listen for the quiet assurance of God's promises.

And then, by placing our lives in His hands, we learn that He is our Shepherd today and throughout eternity. Let us trust the Shepherd.

SOMETHING TO THINK ABOUT

Even when you cannot understand God's plans, you must trust them. If you place yourself in the center of God's will, He will provide for your needs and direct your path.

MORE IDEAS ABOUT
GOD'S WILL

He is the Lord. He will do what He thinks is good.

1 Samuel 3:18 HCSB

Commit your activities to the Lord and your plans will be achieved.

Proverbs 16:3 HCSB

For it is God who is working among you both the willing and the working for His good purpose.

Philippians 2:13 HCSB

Teach me Your way, O Lord; I will walk in Your truth.

Psalm 86:11 NKJV

And do not be conformed to this world, but be transformed by the renewing of your mind, that you may prove what is that good and acceptable and perfect will of God.

Romans 12:2 NKJV

Our sense of joy, satisfaction, and fulfillment in life increases, no matter what the circumstances, if we are in the center of God's will.

Billy Graham

The will of God is never exactly what you expect it to be. It may seem to be much worse, but in the end it's going to be a lot better and a lot bigger.

Elisabeth Elliot

Jesus yielded Himself to the Father's will. He was a model of "reverent submission." Jesus lived a life of prayer, faith, and obedience.

Shirley Dobson

To walk out of His will is to walk into nowhere.

C. S. Lewis

Absolute submission is not enough; we should go on to joyful acquiescence to the will of God.

C. H. Spurgeon

MY THOUGHTS ON . . .
God's will for my life today, this year, and in years to come.

_____

_____

_____

_____

_____

_____

_____

A PRAYER

Lord, give me the wisdom to accept Your will.
When I am confused, give me maturity. When I am worried,
give me perspective. Let me be Your faithful servant,
Father, always seeking Your guidance and Your will for my life.
Amen

Lesson 5

Love Your Neighbors, Even If They're Different

A woman of Samaria came to draw water. "Give Me a drink," Jesus said to her, for His disciples had gone into town to buy food. "How is it that You, a Jew, ask for a drink from me, a Samaritan woman?" she asked. For Jews do not associate with Samaritans. Jesus answered, "If you knew the gift of God, and who is saying to you, 'Give Me a drink,' you would ask Him, and He would give you living water." . . . Now many Samaritans from that town believed in Him because of what the woman said when she testified, "He told me everything I ever did."

John 4:7-11, 39 HCSB

THE LESSON

The woman at the well was so different from most of the women Jesus encountered. She was a Samaritan, and she had been divorced five times. Yet Jesus loved her and validated her life.

There's an old saying that's both familiar and true: If you aren't really loving, you aren't really living. These words, like the familiar text of 1 Corinthians 13:13, remind us of the importance of love. Faith is important, of course. So too is hope. But love is more important still.

Love is a choice. Either you choose to behave lovingly toward others . . . or not; either you behave yourself in ways that enhance your relationships . . . or not. But make no mistake: genuine love requires effort. Simply put, if you wish to build lasting relationships, you must be willing to do your part.

Since the days of Adam and Eve, God has allowed His children to make choices for themselves, and so it is with you. As you interact with family and friends, you have choices to make—lots of choices. If you choose wisely, you'll be rewarded; if you choose unwisely, you'll bear the consequences.

Christ's words are clear: we are to love God first, and secondly, we are to love others as we love ourselves (Matthew 22:37-40). These two commands are seldom easy, and because we are imperfect beings, we often fall short. But God's Holy Word commands us to try.

> Love is the fulfillment of all our works. There is the goal; that is why we run: we run toward it, and once we reach it, in it we shall find rest.
>
> —
>
> *St. Augustine*

The Christian path is an exercise in love and forgiveness. If we are to walk in Christ's footsteps, we must forgive those who have done us harm, and we must accept Christ's love by sharing it freely with family, friends, neighbors, and even strangers.

God does not intend for you to experience mediocre relationships; He created you for far greater things. Building lasting relationships requires compassion, wisdom, empathy, kindness, courtesy, and forgiveness. If that sounds a lot like work, it is—which is perfectly fine with God. Why? Because He knows that you are capable of doing that work, and because He knows that the fruits of your labors will enrich the lives of your loved ones and the lives of generations yet unborn.

SOMETHING TO THINK ABOUT

God is love, and He expects you to share His love with others.

MORE IDEAS ABOUT
LOVING OTHERS

And we have this command from Him: the one who loves God must also love his brother.

1 John 4:21 HCSB

Jesus said to him, "'You shall love the Lord your God with all your heart, with all your soul, and with all your mind.' This is the first and great commandment. And the second is like it: 'You shall love your neighbor as yourself.' On these two commandments hang all the Law and the Prophets."

Matthew 22:37-40 NKJV

Now these three remain: faith, hope, and love. But the greatest of these is love.

1 Corinthians 13:13 HCSB

He who loves his brother abides in the light, and there is no cause for stumbling in him.

1 John 2:10 NKJV

Love one another fervently with a pure heart.

1 Peter 1:22 NKJV

If Jesus is the preeminent One in our lives, then we will love each other, submit to each other, and treat one another fairly in the Lord.

Warren Wiersbe

The truth of the Gospel is intended to free us to love God and others with our whole heart.

John Eldredge

Beware that you are not swallowed up in books! An ounce of love is worth a pound of knowledge.

John Wesley

So Jesus came, stripping himself of everything as he came— omnipotence, omniscience, omnipresence—everything except love. "He emptied himself" (Philippians 2:7), emptied himself of everything except love. Love—his only protection, his only weapon, his only method.

E. Stanley Jones

The world does not understand theology or dogma, but it does understand love and sympathy.

D. L. Moody

When we do little acts of kindness that make life more bearable for someone else, we are walking in love as the Bible commands us.

Barbara Johnson

MY THOUGHTS ON . . .
The people I love most and the ways that I should demonstrate my love for them.

_____

_____

_____

_____

_____

_____

A PRAYER

Lord, You have given me the gift of eternal love; let me share that gift with the world. Help me, Father, to show kindness to those who cross my path, and let me show tenderness and unfailing love to my family and friends. Make me generous with words of encouragement and praise. And, help me always to reflect the love that Christ Jesus gave me so that through me, others might find Him.
Amen

Lesson 6

If You Wish to Follow Jesus, You Must Be a Servant

*Next, He poured water into a basin and began
to wash His disciples' feet and to dry them
with the towel tied around Him.*

John 13:5 HCSB

THE LESSON

Jesus, in one of His last acts here on earth, washed the feet of His disciples. By doing so, He taught them that they, too, must be servants. And, of course, Christ's message still applies.

We live in a world that glorifies power, prestige, fame, and money. But the words of Jesus teach us that the most esteemed men and women are not the widely acclaimed leaders of society; the most esteemed among us are the humble servants of society.

When we experience success, it's easy to puff out our chests and proclaim, "I did that!" But it's wrong. Whatever "it" is, God did it, and He deserves the credit. As Christians, we have been refashioned and saved by Jesus Christ, and that salvation came not because of our own good works but because of God's grace.

Dietrich Bonhoeffer was correct when he observed, "It is very easy to overestimate the importance of our own achievements in comparison with what we owe others." In other words, reality breeds humility.

Are you willing to become a humble servant for Christ? Are you willing to pitch in and make the world a better place, or are you determined to keep all your blessings to yourself? The answer to these questions will determine the quantity and the quality of the service you render to God—and to His children.

Today, you may feel the temptation to take more than you give. You may be tempted to withhold your generosity. Or you may be tempted to build yourself up in the eyes of your friends. Resist these temptations. Instead, serve your

> We worship God through service. The authentic server views each opportunity to lead or serve as an opportunity to worship God.
>
> —
>
> *Bill Hybels*

friends quietly and without fanfare. Find a need and fill it . . . humbly. Lend a helping hand . . . anonymously. Share a word of kindness . . . with quiet sincerity. As you go about your daily activities, remember that the Savior of all humanity made Himself a servant, and you, as His follower, must do no less.

SOMETHING TO THINK ABOUT

Whether you realize it or not, God has called you to a life of service. Your job is to find a place to serve and to get busy.

MORE IDEAS ABOUT
SERVICE

Worship the Lord your God and . . . serve Him only.

Matthew 4:10 HCSB

A person should consider us in this way: as servants of Christ and managers of God's mysteries. In this regard, it is expected of managers that each one be found faithful.

1 Corinthians 4:1-2 HCSB

If they serve Him obediently, they will end their days in prosperity and their years in happiness.

Job 36:11 HCSB

We must do the works of Him who sent Me while it is day. Night is coming when no one can work.

John 9:4 HCSB

Let this mind be in you which was also in Christ Jesus, who . . . made Himself of no reputation, taking the form of a bondservant, and coming in the likeness of men.

Philippians 2:5, 7 NKJV

Through our service to others, God wants to influence our world for Him.

Vonette Bright

God will open up places of service for you as He sees you are ready. Meanwhile, study the Bible and give yourself a chance to grow.

Warren Wiersbe

Christianity, in its purest form, is nothing more than seeing Jesus. Christian service, in its purest form, is nothing more than imitating him who we see. To see his Majesty and to imitate him: that is the sum of Christianity.

Max Lucado

So many times we say that we can't serve God because we aren't whatever is needed. We're not talented enough or smart enough or whatever. But if you are in covenant with Jesus Christ, He is responsible for covering your weaknesses, for being your strength. He will give you His abilities for your disabilities!

Kay Arthur

It is common to think that activity in the service of Christ is the indication of the blessing of God, but be aware of barrenness in a busy life.

Franklin Graham

My Thoughts on . . .
How I can serve God today.

_____

_____

_____

_____

_____

_____

A Prayer

Dear Lord, when Jesus humbled Himself and became a servant,
He also became an example for me. Make me a faithful steward of
my gifts, and let me be a humble servant to my loved ones,
to my friends, and to those in need.
Amen

5-6

Lesson 7

Be an Active Participant in God's Triumphal Church

And I also say to you that you are Peter, and on this rock I will build My church, and the forces of Hades will not overpower it. I will give you the keys of the kingdom of heaven, and whatever you bind on earth will have been bound in heaven, and whatever you loose on earth will have been loosed in heaven.

Matthew 16:18-19 HCSB

THE LESSON

Jesus promised that the church would be triumphant. So, you simply can't go wrong investing your life in His church. The church is eternal.

The Bible teaches that we should worship God in our hearts and in our churches (Acts 20:28). We have clear instructions to "feed the church of God" and to worship our Creator in the presence of fellow believers.

We live in a world that is teeming with temptations and distractions—a world where good and evil struggle in a constant battle to win our minds, our hearts, and our souls. Our challenge, of course, is to ensure that we cast our lot on the side of God. One way that we remain faithful to Him is through the practice of regular, purposeful worship. When we worship the Father faithfully and fervently, we are blessed.

The church belongs to God; it is His just as certainly as we are His. When we help build God's church, we bear witness to the changes that He has made in our lives.

> Christians are like
> coals of a fire.
> Together they glow—
> apart they grow cold.
>
> —
>
> *Anonymous*

Fellowship with other believers should be an integral part of your everyday life. Your association with fellow Christians should be uplifting, enlightening, encouraging, and consistent.

Are you an active member of your own fellowship? Are you a builder of bridges inside the four walls of your church and outside it? Do you contribute to God's glory by contributing your time and your talents to a close-knit band of believers? Hopefully so. The fellowship of believers is intended to be a powerful tool for spreading God's Good News and uplifting His children. And God intends for you to be a fully contributing member of that fellowship. Your intentions should be the same.

SOMETHING TO THINK ABOUT

God wants you to be actively involved in His church.

MORE IDEAS ABOUT CHURCH

For we are God's fellow workers; you are God's field, you are God's building.

1 Corinthians 3:9 NKJV

Now you are the body of Christ, and members individually.

1 Corinthians 12:27 NKJV

Be on guard for yourselves and for all the flock, among whom the Holy Spirit has appointed you as overseers, to shepherd the church of God, which He purchased with His own blood.

Acts 20:28 HCSB

Then He began to teach them: "Is it not written, My house will be called a house of prayer for all nations? . . . "

Mark 11:17 HCSB

For where two or three are gathered together in My name, I am there among them.

Matthew 18:20 HCSB

Our churches are meant to be havens where the caste rules of the world do not apply.

Beth Moore

To model the kingdom of God in the world, the church must not only be a repentant community, committed to truth, but also a holy community.

Chuck Colson

The church is not an end in itself; it is a means to the end of the kingdom of God.

E. Stanley Jones

Every time a new person comes to God, every time someone's gifts find expression in the fellowship of believers, every time a family in need is surrounded by the caring church, the truth is affirmed anew: the Church triumphant is alive and well!

Gloria Gaither

Christians have spent their whole lives mastering all sorts of principles, done their duty, carried on the programs of their church . . . and never known God intimately, heart to heart.

John Eldredge

MY THOUGHTS ON . . .
The role that I can play and should play in my church.

_____

_____

_____

_____

_____

_____

_____

A PRAYER

Dear Lord, today I pray for Your church. Let me help
to feed Your flock by helping to build Your church
so that others, too, might experience Your enduring love
and Your eternal grace.
Amen

Lesson 8

God's Word Is Your Protection Against Temptation

*The Devil said to Him, "I will give You their splendor
and all this authority, because it has been given over
to me, and I can give it to anyone I want.
If You, then, will worship me, all will be Yours."
And Jesus answered him, "It is written:
You shall worship the Lord your God,
and Him alone you shall serve."*

Luke 4:6–8 HCSB

THE LESSON

When the devil himself tried to tempt Jesus, Jesus used the
Word of God as a defense against evil. So can we.

Because our world is filled with temptations, we confront them at every turn. Some of these temptations are small—eating a second piece of chocolate cake, for example. Too much cake may cause us to defile, at least in a modest way, the bodily temple that God has entrusted to our care. But two pieces of cake will not bring us to our knees. Other temptations, however, are not so harmless.

The devil, it seems, is working overtime these days, and causing heartache in more places and in more ways than ever before. We, as Christians, must remain vigilant. Not only must we resist Satan when he confronts us, but we must also avoid those places where Satan can most easily tempt us. And, if we are to avoid the unending temptations of this world, we must arm ourselves with the Word of God.

> We have a decision to make—to turn away from sin or to be miserable and suffer the consequences of continual disobedience.
>
> —
>
> *Vonette Bright*

In a letter to believers, Peter offered a stern warning: "Be sober, be vigilant; because your adversary the devil walks about like a roaring lion, seeking whom he may devour" (1 Peter 5:8 NKJV). What was true in New Testament times is equally true in our own. Satan tempts his prey and then devours them. And in these dangerous times, the tools that Satan uses to destroy his prey are more numerous than ever before.

As believing Christians, we must beware. And, if we seek righteousness in our own lives, we must earnestly wrap ourselves in the protection of God's Holy Word. After fasting forty days and nights in the desert, Jesus Himself was tempted by Satan. Christ used Scripture to rebuke the devil. We must do likewise. The Holy Bible provides us with a perfect blueprint for righteous living. If we consult that blueprint each day and follow its instructions carefully, we build our lives according to God's plan. And when we do, we are secure.

SOMETHING TO THINK ABOUT

Because you live in a temptation-filled world, you must guard your eyes, your thoughts, and your heart—all day, every day.

Number 1 temptation

More Ideas about Temptation

No temptation has overtaken you except what is common to humanity. God is faithful and He will not allow you to be tempted beyond what you are able, but with the temptation He will also provide a way of escape, so that you are able to bear it.

1 Corinthians 10:13 HCSB

Do not be deceived: "Bad company corrupts good morals."

1 Corinthians 15:33 HCSB

Be sober, be vigilant; because your adversary the devil walks about like a roaring lion, seeking whom he may devour.

1 Peter 5:8 NKJV

But the Lord is faithful; He will strengthen and guard you from the evil one.

2 Thessalonians 3:3 HCSB

Blessed is the man who endures temptation; for when he has been approved, he will receive the crown of life which the Lord has promised to those who love Him.

James 1:12 NKJV

Our battles are first won or lost in the secret places of our will in God's presence, never in full view of the world.

Oswald Chambers

A man who gives in to temptation after five minutes simply does not know what it would have been like an hour later.

C. S. Lewis

The only power the devil has is in getting people to believe his lies. If they don't believe his lies, he is powerless to get his work done.

Stormie Omartian

It is easier to stay out of temptation than to get out of it.

Rick Warren

In the worst temptations nothing can help us but faith that God's Son has put on flesh, sits at the right hand of the Father, and prays for us. There is no mightier comfort.

Martin Luther

We, as God's people, are not only to stay far away from sin and sinners who would entice us, but we are to be so like our God that we mourn over sin.

Kay Arthur

dwell in prayer + fellowship

57

MY THOUGHTS ON . . .
How Satan is at work in the world, and how
he can most easily tempt me.

A PRAYER

Dear Lord, this world is filled with temptations, distractions,
and frustrations. When I turn my thoughts away from You and
Your Word, Lord, I suffer bitter consequences. But, when I trust
in Your commandments, I am safe. Direct my path far from the
temptations and distractions of the world. Let me discover
Your will and follow it, Dear Lord, this day and always.
Amen

Lesson 9

Material Possessions
Can Be
Very Dangerous

*"For it is easier for a camel to go through the eye of
a needle than for a rich person to enter
the kingdom of God." Those who heard this asked,
"Then who can be saved?" He replied,
"What is impossible with men is possible with God."*

Luke 18:25-27 HCSB

*(Spiritual possesion
with God*

THE LESSON

Jesus warned against the dangers of materialism, and we must
take His warning seriously.

In our demanding world, financial prosperity can be a good thing, but spiritual prosperity is profoundly more important. Certainly we all need the basic necessities of life, but once we meet those needs for our families and ourselves, the piling up of possessions creates more problems than it solves. Our real riches, of course, are not of this world. We are never really rich until we are rich in spirit. Yet we live in a society that leads us to believe otherwise. The media often glorifies material possessions above all else; God most certainly does not.

Martin Luther observed, "Many things I have tried to grasp and have lost. That which I have placed in God's hands I still have." His words apply to all of us. Our earthly riches are transitory; our spiritual riches, on the other hand, are everlasting.

> Why is love of gold more potent than love of souls?
>
> —
>
> *Lottie Moon*

How much value do you place on your material possessions? And while you're pondering that question, ask yourself this: Do you own your possessions, or vice versa? If you don't like the answer you receive, make an ironclad promise to stop acquiring and start divesting.

Once you stop spending your hard-earned money on frivolous purchases, you'll be amazed at the things you can do without. You'll be pleasantly surprised at the sense of satisfaction that accompanies your newfound moderation. And you'll soon discover that when it comes to material possessions, less truly is more.

Do you find yourself wrapped up in the concerns of the material world? If so, it's time to reorder your priorities and reassess your values. And then, it's time to begin storing up riches that will endure throughout eternity—the spiritual kind.

SOMETHING TO THINK ABOUT

Material possessions may seem appealing at first, but they pale in comparison to the spiritual gifts that God gives to those who put Him first. Count yourself among that number.

More Ideas about Materialism

For where your treasure is, there your heart will be also.

Luke 12:34 NKJV

He who trusts in his riches will fall, but the righteous will flourish . . . .

Proverbs 11:28 NKJV

Do not love the world or the things in the world. If anyone loves the world, the love of the Father is not in him.

1 John 2:15 NKJV

For what does it benefit a man to gain the whole world yet lose his life? What can a man give in exchange for his life?

Mark 8:36-37 HCSB

No man can serve two masters: for either he will hate the one, and love the other; or else he will hold to the one, and despise the other. Ye cannot serve God and mammon.

Matthew 6:24 KJV

Greed is enslaving. The more you have, the more you want—until eventually avarice consumes you.

Kay Arthur

As faithful stewards of what we have, ought we not to give earnest thought to our staggering surplus?

Elisabeth Elliot

The cross is laid on every Christian. It begins with the call to abandon the attachments of this world.

Dietrich Bonhoeffer

There is absolutely no evidence that complexity and materialism lead to happiness. On the contrary, there is plenty of evidence that simplicity and spirituality lead to joy, a blessedness that is better than happiness.

Dennis Swanberg

If you want to be truly happy, you won't find it on an endless quest for more stuff. You'll find it in receiving God's generosity and then passing that generosity along.

Bill Hybels

It's sobering to contemplate how much time, effort, sacrifice, compromise, and attention we give to acquiring and increasing our supply of something that is totally insignificant in eternity.

Anne Graham Lotz

My Thoughts on . . .
The role that material possessions currently play in my life,
and the role that they should play.

_____

_____

_____

_____

_____

_____

_____

_____

A Prayer

Heavenly Father, when I focus intently upon You, I am blessed.
When I focus too intently on the acquisition of material
possessions, I am troubled. Make my priorities pleasing to You,
Father, and make me a worthy servant of Your Son.
Amen

Lesson 10

Use the Talents God Has Given You

His master said to him,
"Well done, good and faithful slave!
You were faithful over a few things; I will put you in
charge of many things. Enter your master's joy!"
Matthew 25:21 HCSB

THE LESSON

In the Parable of the Talents, Jesus instructs us to take the right kinds of risks so that we might enhance our skills and serve our Creator.

God knew precisely what He was doing when He gave you a unique set of talents and opportunities. And now, God wants you to use those talents for the glory of His kingdom. So here's the big question: Will you choose to use those talents, or not?

Your Heavenly Father wants you to be a faithful steward of the gifts He has given you. But you live in a society that may encourage you to do otherwise. You face countless temptations to squander your time, your resources, and your talents. So you must be keenly aware of the inevitable distractions that can waste your time, your energy, and your opportunities.

> God is still in the process of dispensing gifts, and He uses ordinary individuals like us to develop those gifts in other people.
>
> —
>
> *Howard Hendricks*

In the 25th chapter of Matthew, Jesus tells the "Parable of the Talents." In it, He describes a master who leaves his servants with varying amounts of money (talents). When the master returns, some servants have put their money to work and earned more, to which the master responds, "Well done . . . come and share your master's happiness!" (v. 25 NIV)

But the story does not end so happily for the foolish servant who was given a single talent but did nothing with it. For this man, the master has nothing but reproach: "You wicked, lazy servant . . ." (v. 26 NIV). The message from Jesus is clear: We must use our talents, not waste them.

Every day of your life, you have a choice to make: to nurture your talents or neglect them. When you choose wisely, God rewards your efforts, and He expands your opportunities to serve Him.

God has blessed you with unique opportunities to serve Him, and He has given you every tool that you need to do so. Today, accept this challenge: value the talent that God has given you, nourish it, make it grow, and share it with the world. After all, the best way to say "Thank You" for God's gifts is to use them.

SOMETHING TO THINK ABOUT

If you are a disciple of the risen Christ, you have every reason on earth—and in heaven—to live courageously. And that's precisely what you should do.

MORE IDEAS ABOUT TALENTS

According to the grace given to us, we have different gifts: If prophecy, use it according to the standard of faith; if service, in service; if teaching, in teaching; if exhorting, in exhortation; giving, with generosity; leading, with diligence; showing mercy, with cheerfulness.

Romans 12:6-8 HCSB

Do not neglect the gift that is in you.

1 Timothy 4:14 HCSB

Each one has his own gift from God, one in this manner and another in that.

1 Corinthians 7:7 NKJV

I remind you to keep ablaze the gift of God that is in you.

2 Timothy 1:6 HCSB

Based on the gift they have received, everyone should use it to serve others, as good managers of the varied grace of God.

1 Peter 4:10 HCSB

Employ whatever God has entrusted you with, in doing good, all possible good, in every possible kind and degree.

John Wesley

If you want to reach your potential, you need to add a strong work ethic to your talent.

John Maxwell

God often reveals His direction for our lives through the way He made us . . . with a certain personality and unique skills.

Bill Hybels

Almighty God created us, redeemed us, called us, endowed us with gifts and abilities and perceptions. To demean the gift is to insult the Giver.

Penelope Stokes

One thing taught large in the Holy Scriptures is that while God gives His gifts freely, He will require a strict accounting of them at the end of the road. Each man is personally responsible for his store, be it large or small, and will be required to explain his use of it before the judgment seat of Christ.

A. W. Tozer

God has given you special talents—now it's your turn to give them back to God.

Marie T. Freeman

MY THOUGHTS ON . . .
Ways that I can use my talents today, tomorrow,
and in years to come.

_____

_____

_____

_____

_____

_____

_____

_____

A PRAYER

Lord, You have given all of us talents, and I am no exception.
You have blessed me with a gift—let me discover it,
nurture it, and use it for the glory of Your Kingdom.
I will share my gifts with the world, and I will praise You,
the Giver of all things good.
Amen

July 8th

Lesson 11

Your Search for Meaning Must Include God

"I am the bread of life," Jesus told them.
"No one who comes to Me will ever be hungry,
and no one who believes in Me will ever be thirsty again."
John 6:35 HCSB

THE LESSON

Jesus said that He was the answer to man's search for meaning and significance.

The sooner we discover what God intends for us to do with our days, the better. But God's purposes aren't always clear to us. Sometimes we wander aimlessly in a spiritual desert of our own making. And sometimes, we struggle stubbornly against God in a futile effort to discover fulfillment and happiness through our own means, not His.

Whenever we resist God's purposes, we are frustrated, and our efforts bear little fruit. But when we genuinely seek His wisdom—and when we follow God's Son wherever He chooses to lead us—the Creator blesses us in unexpected ways.

> Without God,
> life has no purpose,
> and without purpose,
> life has no meaning.
>
> —
>
> *Rick Warren*

How can we know precisely what God's intentions are? The answer, of course, is that we can't always know exactly what God intends for us to do. Even the most saintly among us will experience periods of uncertainty and doubt. Sometimes, outside circumstances will force us to reevaluate our lives; on other occasions, we may become frustrated, not by the turbulence of life, but by its sameness. In either case, we may find ourselves searching for new direction. If we are wise, we turn to God for that direction.

Are you earnestly seeking to discern God's plans and purposes for your life? If so, remember these important facts:

1. God has wonderful plans in store for you;
2. If you petition God sincerely and prayerfully, you will discern His will;
3. When you discover God's purpose for your life, you will experience abundance, peace, fulfillment, and joy.

And rest assured: when God's purpose becomes your purpose, He will bless you, He will use you, and He will keep you—now and forever.

SOMETHING TO THINK ABOUT

When you gain a clear vision of your purpose for life here on earth—and for life everlasting—your steps will be sure.

More Ideas about Purpose

Whatever you do, do all to the glory of God.

1 Corinthians 10:31 NKJV

To everything there is a season, a time for every purpose under heaven.

Ecclesiastes 3:1 NKJV

For we are His making, created in Christ Jesus for good works, which God prepared ahead of time so that we should walk in them.

Ephesians 2:10 HCSB

For it is God who is working among you both the willing and the working for His good purpose.

Philippians 2:13 HCSB

You will show me the path of life; in Your presence is fullness of joy; at Your right hand are pleasures forevermore.

Psalm 16:11 NKJV

Continually restate to yourself what the purpose of your life is.

Oswald Chambers

When God speaks to you through the Bible, prayer, circumstances, the church, or in some other way, he has a purpose in mind for your life.

Henry Blackaby and Claude King

God wants to revolutionize our lives—by showing us how knowing Him can be the most powerful force to help us become all we want to be.

Bill Hybels

Whatever purpose motivates your life, it must be something big enough and grand enough to make the investment worthwhile.

Warren Wiersbe

The worst thing that laziness does is rob a man of spiritual purpose.

Billy Graham

A fish would never be happy living on land, because it was made for water. An eagle could never feel satisfied if it wasn't allowed to fly. You will never feel completely satisfied on earth, because you were made for more.

Rick Warren

MY THOUGHTS ON . . .
My purpose for living and my passion for life.

_____

_____

_____

_____

_____

_____

_____

A PRAYER

Dear Lord, I know that You have a purpose for my life,
and I will seek that purpose today and every day that I live.
Let my actions be pleasing to You, and let me share
Your Good News with a world that so desperately needs
Your healing hand and the salvation of Your Son.
Amen

Lesson 12

Take Time to Recharge Your Batteries

Come to Me, all you who are weary and burdened,
and I will give you rest. Take My yoke upon you
and learn from Me, because I am gentle
and humble in heart, and you will find rest for your souls.
For My yoke is easy and My burden is light.

Matthew 11:28-30 HCSB

THE LESSON

Jesus offers peace and rest. Jesus brings simplicity. Jesus is the answer to exhaustion and burnout.

Physical exhaustion is God's way of telling us to slow down. God expects us to work hard, of course, but He also intends for us to rest. When we fail to take the rest that we need, we do a disservice to ourselves and to our families.

We live in a world that tempts us to stay up late—very late. But too much late-night TV, combined with too little sleep, is a prescription for exhaustion.

Jesus promises us that when we come to Him, He will give us rest—but we, too, must do our part. We must take the necessary steps to insure that we have sufficient rest and that we take care of our bodies in other ways, too.

As adults, each of us bears a personal responsibility for the general state of our own physical health. Certainly, various aspects of health are beyond our control: illness sometimes strikes even the healthiest men and women. But for most of us, physical health is a choice: it is the result of hundreds of small decisions that we make every day of our lives. If we make decisions that promote good health, our bodies respond. But if we fall into bad habits and undisciplined lifestyles, we suffer tragic consequences.

> Notice what Jesus had to say concerning those who have wearied themselves by trying to do things in their own strength: "Come to me, all you who labor and are heavy laden, and I will give you rest."
>
> —
>
> *Henry Blackaby and Claude King*

Are your physical or spiritual batteries running low? Is your energy on the wane? Are your emotions frayed? If so, it's time to turn your thoughts and your prayers to God's Son. And when you're finished, it's probably time to turn off the lights and go to bed!

SOMETHING TO THINK ABOUT

God wants you to get enough rest. The world wants you to burn the candle at both ends. Trust God.

MORE IDEAS ABOUT
REST

And the apostles gathered themselves together unto Jesus, and told him all things, both what they had done, and what they had taught. And he said unto them, Come ye yourselves apart into a desert place, and rest a while.

Mark 6:30-31 HCSB

He makes me to lie down in green pastures; He leads me beside the still waters. He restores my soul; He leads me in the paths of righteousness for His name's sake.

Psalm 23:2-3 NKJV

Return to your rest, O my soul, for the LORD has dealt bountifully with you.

Psalm 116:7 NKJV

Rest in God alone, my soul, for my hope comes from Him.

Psalm 62:5 HCSB

And you would be secure, because there is hope; Yes, you would dig around you, and take your rest in safety.

Job 11:18 NKJV

Jesus gives us the ultimate rest, the confidence we need, to escape the frustration and chaos of the world around us.

Billy Graham

Satan does some of his worst work on exhausted Christians when nerves are frayed and their minds are faint.

Vance Havner

Jesus taught us by example to get out of the rat race and recharge our batteries.

Barbara Johnson

Life is strenuous. See that your clock does not run down.

Mrs. Charles E. Cowman

One reason so much American Christianity is a mile wide and an inch deep is that Christians are simply tired. Sometimes you need to kick back and rest for Jesus' sake.

Dennis Swanberg

Come, come, come unto Me, weary and sore distressed; come, come, come unto Me, come unto Me and rest.

Fanny Crosby

MY THOUGHTS ON . . .
Ways that I can improve my spiritual, emotional,
and physical health.

_____

_____

_____

_____

_____

_____

_____

A PRAYER

Dear Lord, You can make all things new. I am a new creature
in Christ Jesus, and when I fall short in my commitment,
You can renew my effort and my enthusiasm.
When I am weak or worried, restore my strength, Lord,
for my own sake and for the sake of Your kingdom.
Amen

Lesson 13

Be Compassionate

Just as you want others to do for you,
do the same for them.
Luke 6:31 HCSB

THE LESSON

Jesus was compassionate, and He commanded us to follow His example.

John Wesley's advice was straightforward: "Do all the good you can. By all the means you can. In all the ways you can. In all the places you can. At all the times you can. To all the people you can. As long as ever you can." One way to do all the good you can is to spread kindness wherever you go.

Sometimes, when we feel happy or generous, we find it easy to be compassionate. Other times, when we are discouraged or tired, we can scarcely summon the energy to utter a single kind word. But, God's commandment is clear: He intends that we make the conscious choice to treat others with kindness and respect, no matter our circumstances, no matter our emotions.

> When you launch an act of kindness out into the crosswinds of life, it will blow kindness back to you.
>
> —
>
> *Dennis Swanberg*

St. Teresa of Avila observed, "There are only two duties required of us—the love of God and the love of our neighbor, and the surest sign of discovering whether we observe these duties is the love of our neighbor." Her words remind us that we honor God by serving our friends and neighbors with kind words, heartfelt prayers, and helping hands. If we sincerely desire to follow in the footsteps of God's Son, we must make kindness and generosity the hallmark of our dealings with others.

Do you look for opportunities to share God's love with your family and friends? Hopefully you do. After all, your Heavenly Father has blessed you in countless ways, and He has instructed you to share your blessings with the world. So today, look for opportunities to spread kindness wherever you go. God deserves no less, and neither, for that matter, do your loved ones.

SOMETHING TO THINK ABOUT

Compassionate words and deeds have echoes that last a lifetime and beyond.

MORE IDEAS ABOUT
COMPASSION

Finally, all of you be of one mind, having compassion for one another; love as brothers, be tenderhearted, be courteous.

1 Peter 3:8 NKJV

Therefore, God's chosen ones, holy and loved, put on heartfelt compassion, kindness, humility, gentleness, and patience.

Colossians 3:12 HCSB

And be kind and compassionate to one another, forgiving one another, just as God also forgave you in Christ.

Ephesians 4:32 HCSB

Pure and undefiled religion before our God and Father is this: to look after orphans and widows in their distress and to keep oneself unstained by the world.

James 1:27 HCSB

Assuredly, I say to you, inasmuch as you did it to one of the least of these My brethren, you did it to Me.

Matthew 25:40 NKJV

When action-oriented compassion is absent, it's a tell-tale sign that something's spiritually amiss.

Bill Hybels

Our Lord worked with people as they were, and He was patient—not tolerant of sin, but compassionate.

Vance Havner

If we have the true love of God in our hearts, we will show it in our lives. We will not have to go up and down the earth proclaiming it. We will show it in everything we say or do.

D. L. Moody

A little kindly advice is better than a great deal of scolding.

Fanny Crosby

Kindness in this world will do much to help others, not only to come into the light, but also to grow in grace day by day.

Fanny Crosby

It is one of the most beautiful compensations of life that no one can sincerely try to help another without helping herself.

Barbara Johnson

MY THOUGHTS ON . . .
Ways that I can share kind words and kind deeds today.

_____

_____

_____

_____

_____

_____

_____

A PRAYER

Help me, Lord, to see the needs of those around me.
Today, let me show courtesy to those who cross my path.
Today, let me spread kind words in honor of Your Son.
Today, let forgiveness rule my heart. And every day, Lord,
let my love for Christ be demonstrated through the acts
of kindness that I offer to those who need
the healing touch of the Master's hand.
Amen

July 29th

Lesson 14

Real Christianity Requires Obedience to God

Not everyone who says to Me, "Lord, Lord,"
shall enter the kingdom of heaven, but he who does
the will of My Father in heaven.

Matthew 7:21 NKJV

THE LESSON

Jesus warns us that while many people may call His name, only those who obey God will follow in Christ's footsteps.

Obedience to God is determined, not by our words, but by our deeds. Talking about righteousness is easy; living righteously is far more difficult, especially in today's temptation-filled world.

Since God created Adam and Eve, we human beings have been rebelling against our Creator. Why? Because we are unwilling to trust God's Word, and we are unwilling to follow His commandments. God has given us a guidebook for righteous living called the Holy Bible. It contains thorough instructions which, if followed, lead to fulfillment, abundance, and salvation. But, if we choose to ignore God's commandments, the results are as predictable as they are tragic.

In Ephesians 2:10 we read, "For we are His workmanship, created in Christ Jesus for good works" (NKJV). These words are instructive: We are not saved by good works, but for good works. Good works are not the root, but rather the fruit of our salvation.

When we seek righteousness in our own lives—and when we seek the companionship of those who do likewise—we reap the spiritual rewards that God intends for our lives. When we behave ourselves as godly men and women, we honor God. When we live righteously and according to God's commandments, He blesses us in ways that we cannot fully understand.

> Let your fellowship with the Father and with the Lord Jesus Christ have as its one aim and object a life of quiet, determined, unquestioning obedience.
>
> —
>
> *Andrew Murray*

Do you seek God's peace and His blessings? Then obey Him. When you're faced with a difficult choice or a powerful temptation, seek God's counsel and trust the counsel He gives. Invite God into your heart and live according to His commandments. When you do, you will be blessed today and tomorrow and forever.

How to stay obedient
1) Eyes on God
2) Pray
3) Stay in his word

SOMETHING TO THINK ABOUT

When you are obedient to God, you are secure; when you are not, you are not.

MORE IDEAS ABOUT OBEDIENCE

I have sought You with all my heart; don't let me wander from Your commands.

Psalm 119:10 HCSB

Therefore, everyone who hears these words of Mine and acts on them will be like a sensible man who built his house on the rock. The rain fell, the rivers rose, and the winds blew and pounded that house. Yet it didn't collapse, because its foundation was on the rock.

Matthew 7:24–25 HCSB

And the world with its lust is passing away, but the one who does God's will remains forever.

1 John 2:17 HCSB

But whoever keeps His word, truly the love of God is perfected in him. By this we know that we are in Him. He who says he abides in Him ought himself also to walk just as He walked.

1 John 2:5-6 NKJV

Rest your hope fully upon the grace that is to be brought to you at the revelation of Jesus Christ; as obedient children, not conforming yourselves to the former lusts, as in your ignorance; but as He who called you is holy, you also be holy in all your conduct.

1 Peter 1:13-15 NKJV

True faith commits us to obedience.

A. W. Tozer

Let us never suppose that obedience is impossible or that holiness is meant only for a select few. Our Shepherd leads us in paths of righteousness—not for our name's sake but for His.

Elisabeth Elliot

When you suffer and lose, that does not mean you are being disobedient to God. In fact, it might mean you're right in the center of His will. The path of obedience is often marked by times of suffering and loss.

Charles Swindoll

Trials and sufferings teach us to obey the Lord by faith, and we soon learn that obedience pays off in joyful ways.

Bill Bright

Obedience is the road to freedom, humility the road to pleasure, unity the road to personality.

C. S. Lewis

Perfect obedience would be perfect happiness, if only we had perfect confidence in the power we were obeying.

Corrie ten Boom

MY THOUGHTS ON . . .
The wisdom of being obedient to God.

_____

_____

_____

_____

_____

_____

_____

A PRAYER

Dear Lord, today, I will embrace Your love and accept
Your wisdom. Guide me, Father, and deliver me from
the painful mistakes that I make when I stray from
Your commandments. Let me live by Your Word,
and let me grow in my faith every day that I live.
Amen

Aug 5th

Lesson 15

Miracles Happen

*And immediately Jesus stretched out His hand
and caught him, and said to him,
"O you of little faith, why did you doubt?"*

Matthew 14:31 NKJV

THE LESSON

To do miraculous things, you need faith. To do the impossible,
you must stay focused on Jesus and have faith in Him.

Jesus performed many miracles, and we still live in a world where miracles are taking place all around us. But sometimes, because of limited faith and limited understanding, we wrongly assume that God cannot or will not intervene in the affairs of mankind. Such assumptions are simply wrong.

Are you afraid to ask God to do big things in your life? Is your faith threadbare and worn? If so, it's time to abandon your doubts and reclaim your faith—faith in yourself, faith in your abilities, faith in your future, and faith in your Heavenly Father.

> We have a God
> who delights
> in impossibilities.
>
> —
>
> *Andrew Murray*

Catherine Marshall notes that, "God specializes in things thought impossible." And make no mistake: God can help you do things you never dreamed possible . . . your job is to let Him.

Sometimes, when we read of God's miraculous works in Biblical times, we tell ourselves, "That was then, but this is now." When we do so, we are mistaken. God is with His children "now" just as He was "then." He is right here, right now, performing miracles. And, He will continue to work miracles in our lives to the extent we are willing to trust in Him and to the extent those miracles fit into the fabric of His divine plan.

Miracles—both great and small—happen around us all day every day, but usually, we're too busy to notice. Some miracles, like the twinkling of a star or the glory of a sunset, we take for granted. Other miracles, like the healing of a terminally sick patient, we chalk up to fate or to luck. We assume, quite incorrectly, that God is "out there" and we are "right here." Nothing could be farther from the truth.

Do you lack the faith that God can work miracles in your own life? If so, it's time to reconsider. Instead of doubting God, trust His power, and expect His miracles. Then, wait patiently . . . because something miraculous is about to happen.

Be obedient to God

SOMETHING TO THINK ABOUT

God does miraculous things, so you should never be afraid to ask Him to perform a miracle.

MORE IDEAS ABOUT
MIRACLES

Looking at them, Jesus said, "With men it is impossible, but not with God, because all things are possible with God."

Mark 10:27 HCSB

I assure you: The one who believes in Me will also do the works that I do. And he will do even greater works than these, because I am going to the Father.

John 14:12 HCSB

For with God nothing will be impossible.

Luke 1:37 NKJV

But Jesus looked at them and said, "With men this is impossible, but with God all things are possible."

Matthew 19:26 HCSB

You are the God who does wonders; You have declared Your strength among the peoples.

Psalm 77:14 NKJV

The miracles in fact are a retelling in small letters of the very same story which is written across the whole world in letters too large for some of us to see.

C. S. Lewis

When God is involved, anything can happen. Be open and stay that way. God has a beautiful way of bringing good vibrations out of broken chords.

Charles Swindoll

When we face an impossible situation, all self-reliance and self-confidence must melt away; we must be totally dependent on Him for the resources.

Anne Graham Lotz

Only God can move mountains, but faith and prayer can move God.

E. M. Bounds

God specializes in things thought impossible.

Catherine Marshall

Miracles are not contrary to nature but only contrary to what we know about nature.

St. Augustine

MY THOUGHTS ON . . .

Whether or not I'm really attuned to the miracles
that God is performing every day.

_____

_____

_____

_____

_____

_____

_____

A PRAYER

Dear Lord, keep me always mindful of Your strength.
When I lose hope, give me faith; when others lose hope,
let me tell them of Your glory and Your works.
Because nothing is impossible for You,
I will pray for miracles . . . and I will work for them.
Amen

Lesson 16

Forgiveness
Is Not Optional

Then Jesus said, "Father, forgive them,
for they do not know what they do."
And they divided His garments and cast lots.

Luke 23:34 NKJV

THE LESSON

Even while He endured the pain of the crucifixion, Jesus
would not withhold forgiveness from the men who were killing
Him. Jesus was—and is—a model of forgiveness.

It has been said that life is an exercise in forgiveness. How true. Christ understood the importance of forgiveness when He commanded, "Love your enemies and pray for those who persecute you" (Matthew 5:43-44 NIV). But sometimes, forgiveness is difficult indeed.

When we have been injured or embarrassed, we feel the urge to strike back and to hurt the ones who have hurt us. But Christ instructs us to do otherwise. Christ teaches us that forgiveness is God's way and that mercy is an integral part of God's plan for our lives. In short, we are commanded to weave the thread of forgiveness into the very fabric of our lives.

> Our forgiveness toward others should flow from a realization and appreciation of God's forgiveness toward us.
>
> —
>
> *Franklin Graham*

Do you invest more time than you should reliving the past? Are you troubled by feelings of anger, bitterness, envy, or regret? Do you harbor ill will against someone whom you simply can't seem to forgive? If so, it's time to finally get serious about forgiveness.

When someone hurts you, the act of forgiveness is difficult, but necessary. Until you forgive, you are trapped in a prison of your own creation. But what if you have tried to forgive and simply can't seem to do so? The solution to your dilemma is this: you must make forgiveness a higher priority in your life.

Most of us don't spend much time thinking about forgiveness; we worry, instead, about the injustices we have suffered and the people who inflicted them. God has a better plan: He wants us to live in the present, not the past, and He knows that in order to do so, we must forgive those who have harmed us.

Have you made forgiveness a high priority? Have you sincerely asked God to forgive you for your inability to forgive others? Have you genuinely prayed that those feelings of hatred and anger might be swept from your heart? If so, congratulations. If not, perhaps it's time to rearrange your priorities . . . and perhaps it's time to free yourself from the chains of bitterness and regret.

SOMETHING TO THINK ABOUT

God's Word instructs you to forgive others . . . no exceptions.

MORE IDEAS ABOUT
FORGIVENESS

All bitterness, anger and wrath, insult and slander must be removed from you, along with all wickedness. And be kind and compassionate to one another, forgiving one another, just as God also forgave you in Christ.

Ephesians 4:31-32 HCSB

See to it that no one repays evil for evil to anyone, but always pursue what is good for one another and for all.

1 Thessalonians 5:15 HCSB

He who says he is in the light, and hates his brother, is in darkness until now.

1 John 2:9 NKJV

If anyone says, "I love God," yet hates his brother, he is a liar. For the person who does not love his brother whom he has seen cannot love God whom he has not seen. And we have this command from Him: the one who loves God must also love his brother.

1 John 4:20-21 HCSB

But the wisdom from above is first pure, then peace-loving, gentle, compliant, full of mercy and good fruits, without favoritism and hypocrisy.

James 3:17 HCSB

As you have received the mercy of God by the forgiveness of sin and the promise of eternal life, thus you must show mercy.

Billy Graham

Only the truly forgiven are truly forgiving.

C. S. Lewis

If God has truly forgiven you then you are forgiven

Our relationships with other people are of primary importance to God. Because God is love, He cannot tolerate any unforgiveness or hardness in us toward any individual.

Catherine Marshall

Forgiveness is not an emotion. Forgiveness is an act of the will, and the will can function regardless of the temperature of the heart.

Corrie ten Boom

Revenge is the raging fire that consumes the arsonist.

Max Lucado

We cannot out-sin God's ability to forgive us.

Beth Moore

105

MY THOUGHTS ON . . .
The people whom I still need to forgive.

_____

_____

_____

_____

_____

_____

_____

A PRAYER

Dear Lord, when I am bitter, You can change
my unforgiving heart. When I am slow to forgive,
Your Word reminds me that forgiveness is Your commandment.
Let me be Your obedient servant, Lord, and let me forgive
others just as You have forgiven me.
Amen

Lesson 17

You Can Find Joy in Christ

I have spoken these things to you so that
My joy may be in you and your joy may be complete.
John 15:11 HCSB

THE LESSON

Joy is found in Jesus—knowing Him, loving Him, and serving Him. He is the vine and we are the branches.

Have you made the choice to rejoice? If you're a Christian, you have every reason to be joyful. After all, the ultimate battle has already been won on the cross at Calvary. And if your life has been transformed by Christ's sacrifice, then you, as a recipient of God's grace, have every reason to live joyfully. Yet sometimes, amid the inevitable hustle and bustle of life here on earth, you may lose sight of your blessings as you wrestle with the challenges of everyday life.

Do you seek happiness, abundance, and contentment? If so, here are some things you should do: Love God and His Son; depend upon God for strength; try, to the best of your abilities, to follow God's will; and strive to obey His Holy Word. When you do these things, you'll discover that happiness goes hand-in-hand with righteousness. The happiest people are not those who rebel against God; the happiest people are those who love God and obey His commandments.

> Joy is the direct result of having God's perspective on our daily lives and the effect of loving our Lord enough to obey His commands and trust His promises.
>
> —
>
> *Bill Bright*

What does life have in store for you? A world full of possibilities (of course it's up to you to seize them) and God's promise of abundance (of course it's up to you to accept it). So, as you embark upon the next phase of your journey, remember to celebrate the life that God has given you. Your Creator has blessed you beyond measure. Honor Him with your prayers, your words, your deeds, and your joy.

SOMETHING TO THINK ABOUT

Joy begins with a choice—the choice to establish a genuine relationship with God and His Son. Joy does not depend upon your circumstances, but upon your relationship with God.

MORE IDEAS ABOUT
JOY

Weeping may spend the night, but there is joy in the morning.

Psalm 30:5 HCSB

A joyful heart is good medicine, but a broken spirit dries up the bones.

Proverbs 17:22 HCSB

Make a joyful shout to the LORD, all you lands! Serve the LORD with gladness; come before His presence with singing.

Psalm 100:1-2 NKJV

Now I am coming to You, and I speak these things in the world so that they may have My joy completed in them.

John 17:13 HCSB

Until now you have asked for nothing in My name. Ask and you will receive, that your joy may be complete.

John 16:24 HCSB

Our sense of joy, satisfaction, and fulfillment in life increases, no matter what the circumstances, if we are in the center of God's will.

Billy Graham

Joy is the heart's harmonious response to the Lord's song of love.

A. W. Tozer

A life of intimacy with God is characterized by joy.

Oswald Chambers

Rejoice, the Lord is King; Your Lord and King adore! Rejoice, give thanks and sing and triumph evermore.

Charles Wesley

How changed our lives would be if we could only fly through the days on wings of surrender and trust!

Hannah Whitall Smith

Joy in life is not the absence of sorrow. The fact that Jesus could have joy in the midst of sorrow is proof that we can experience this too.

Warren Wiersbe

MY THOUGHTS ON . . .
My need to celebrate life today.

_____

_____

_____

_____

_____

_____

_____

A PRAYER

Dear Lord, You are my loving Heavenly Father,
and You created me in Your image. As Your faithful child,
I will make Your joy my joy. I will praise Your works,
I will obey Your Word, and I will honor Your Son,
this day and every day of my life.
Amen

Lesson 18

You Can Tap in to God's Power

But you will receive power when the Holy Spirit has come upon you, and you will be My witnesses in Jerusalem, in all Judea and Samaria, and to the ends of the earth.

Acts 1:8 HCSB

THE LESSON

Jesus promised that He would give us the strength to do His work. Our task is to accept God's power and use it for His kingdom.

Even the most inspired Christians can, from time to time, find themselves running on empty. The demands of daily life can drain us of our strength and rob us of the joy that is rightfully ours in Christ. When we find ourselves tired, discouraged, or worse, there is a source from which we can draw the power needed to recharge our spiritual batteries. That source is God.

God intends that His children lead joyous lives filled with abundance and peace. But sometimes, abundance and peace seem very far away. It is then that we must turn to God for renewal, and when we do, He will restore us if we allow Him to do so.

Today, like every other day, is literally brimming with possibilities. Whether we realize it or not, God is always working in us and through us; our job is to let Him do His work without undue interference. Yet we are imperfect beings who, because of our limited vision, often resist God's will. And oftentimes, because of our stubborn insistence on squeezing too many activities into a 24-hour day, we allow ourselves to become exhausted or frustrated, or both.

> When God is our strength, it is strength indeed; when our strength is our own, it is only weakness.
>
> —
>
> *St. Augustine*

Are you tired or troubled? Turn your heart toward God in prayer. Are you weak or worried? Take the time—or, more accurately, make the time—to delve deeply into God's Holy Word. Are you spiritually depleted? Call upon fellow believers to support you, and call upon Christ to renew your spirit and your life. Are you simply overwhelmed by the demands of the day? Pray for the wisdom to simplify your life. Are you exhausted? Pray for the wisdom to rest a little more and worry a little less.

When you do these things, you'll discover that the Creator of the universe stands always ready and always able to create a new sense of wonderment and joy in you.

SOMETHING TO THINK ABOUT

When you are tired, fearful, or discouraged, God can restore your strength.

MORE IDEAS ABOUT STRENGTH

And He said to me, "My grace is sufficient for you, for My strength is made perfect in weakness."

2 Corinthians 12:9 NKJV

You, therefore, my child, be strong in the grace that is in Christ Jesus.

2 Timothy 2:1 HCSB

God is our refuge and strength, a very present help in trouble.

Psalm 46:1 NKJV

I can do all things through Christ who strengthens me.

Philippians 4:13 NKJV

But those who wait on the Lord shall renew their strength; they shall mount up with wings like eagles, they shall run and not be weary, they shall walk and not faint.

Isaiah 40:31 NKJV

No matter how heavy the burden, daily strength is given, so I expect we need not give ourselves any concern as to what the outcome will be. We must simply go forward.

Annie Armstrong

God conquers only what we yield to Him. Yet, when He does, and when our surrender is complete, He fills us with a new strength that we could never have known by ourselves. His conquest is our victory!

Shirley Dobson

A divine strength is given to those who yield themselves to the Father and obey what He tells them to do.

Warren Wiersbe

The amount of power you experience to live a victorious, triumphant Christian life is directly proportional to the freedom you give the Spirit to be Lord of your life!

Anne Graham Lotz

You needn't worry about not feeling brave. Our Lord didn't—see the scene in Gethsemane. How thankful I am that when God became man He did not choose to become a man of iron nerves; that would not have helped weaklings like you and me nearly so much.

C. S. Lewis

MY THOUGHTS ON . . .
The strength that is mine when I follow God's path
and trust His promises.

A PRAYER

Lord, sometimes life is difficult. Sometimes, I am worried,
weary, or heartbroken. But, when I lift my eyes to You, Father,
You strengthen me. When I am weak, You lift me up.
Today, I turn to You, Lord, for my strength,
for my hope, and my salvation.
Amen

Lesson 19

Be Loyal to God

By Being in his Word   Prayer, Faith HolySpirit

"Follow Me," Jesus told them,
"and I will make you into fishers of men!"
Immediately they left their nets and followed Him.

Mark 1:17-18 HCSB

THE LESSON

Christ's instructions were clear: His disciples were to give Him their undivided loyalty. And so must we.

When Jesus addressed His disciples, He warned that each one must "take up his cross and follow me." The disciples must have known exactly what the Master meant. In Jesus' day, prisoners were forced to carry their own crosses to the location where they would be put to death. Thus, Christ's message was clear: in order to follow Him, Christ's disciples must deny themselves and, instead, trust Him completely. Nothing has changed since then.

> What our Lord said about cross-bearing and obedience is not in fine type. It is in bold print on the face of the contract.
>
> —
>
> *Vance Havner*

If we are to be disciples of Christ, we must trust Him and place Him at the very center of our beings. Jesus never comes "next." He is always first. The paradox, of course, is that only by sacrificing ourselves to Him do we gain salvation for ourselves.

Jesus has called upon believers of every generation (and that includes you) to walk with Him. Jesus promises that when you follow in His footsteps, He will teach you how to live freely and lightly (Matthew 11:28-30). And when Jesus makes a promise, you can depend upon it.

Are you worried or anxious? Be confident in the power of Christ. He will never desert you. Are you discouraged? Be courageous and call upon your Savior. He will protect you and use you according to His purposes. Do you seek to be a worthy disciple of the One from Galilee? Then pick up His cross today and every day of your life. When you do, He will bless you now . . . and forever.

What we sacrifice
Money
Time
The Right to be right
Turn the other cheek
Family Relationships

SOMETHING TO THINK ABOUT

Jesus has invited you to become His disciple. If you accept His invitation—and if you obey His commandments—you will be protected and blessed.

Be loyal
Trust him

MORE IDEAS ABOUT DISCIPLESHIP

But whoever keeps His word, truly in him the love of God is perfected. This is how we know we are in Him: the one who says he remains in Him should walk just as He walked.

1 John 2:5-6 HCSB

You did not choose Me, but I chose you. I appointed you that you should go out and produce fruit, and that your fruit should remain, so that whatever you ask the Father in My name, He will give you.

John 15:16 HCSB

"While you have the light, believe in the light, that you may become sons of light." These things Jesus spoke, and departed, and was hidden from them.

John 12:36 NKJV

Then Jesus said to His disciples, "If anyone wants to come with Me, he must deny himself, take up his cross, and follow Me."

Matthew 16:24 HCSB

He has shown you, O man, what is good; and what does the LORD require of you but to do justly, to love mercy, and to walk humbly with your God?

Micah 6:8 NKJV

In our faith we follow in someone's steps. In our faith we leave footprints to guide others. It's the principle of discipleship.

Max Lucado

A disciple is a follower of Christ. That means you take on His priorities as your own. His agenda becomes your agenda. His mission becomes your mission.

Charles Stanley

As we seek to become disciples of Jesus Christ, we should never forget that the word *disciple* is directly related to the word *discipline*. To be a disciple of the Lord Jesus Christ is to know his discipline.

Dennis Swanberg

A follower is never greater than his leader; a follower never draws attention to himself.

Franklin Graham

It is the secret of true discipleship to bear the cross, to acknowledge the death sentence that has been passed on self, and to deny any right that self has to rule over us.

Andrew Murray

MY THOUGHTS ON . . .
Steps that I can take today to be a better disciple of Christ.

_____

_____

_____

_____

_____

_____

_____

A PRAYER

Dear Lord, thank You for the gift of Your Son Jesus.
Let me be a worthy disciple of Christ, and let me be ever
grateful for His love. I offer my life to You, Lord, so that I might
live according to Your commandments and according to
Your plan. I will praise You always as I give thanks for
Your Son and for Your everlasting love. .
Amen

Lesson 20

You Can Find Peace

Peace I leave with you. My peace I give to you.
I do not give to you as the world gives.
Your heart must not be troubled or fearful.

John 14:27 HCSB

THE LESSON

Jesus can quiet the storms of life—it is our responsibility to let Him.

Have you found the lasting peace that can—and should—be yours through Jesus Christ? Or are you still chasing the illusion of "peace and happiness" that the world promises but cannot deliver?

The beautiful words of John 14:27 promise that Jesus offers peace, not as the world gives, but as He alone gives. Your challenge is to welcome Christ's peace into your heart and then, as best you can, to share His peace with your neighbors. But sometimes, that's easier said than done.

If you are a person with lots of obligations and plenty of responsibilities, it is simply a fact of life: You worry. From time to time, you worry about finances, safety, health, home, family, or about countless other concerns, some great and some small. Where is the best place to take your worries? Take them to God . . . and leave them there.

> Trade God your pieces
> for His peace.
>
> —
>
> *Anonymous*

The Scottish preacher George MacDonald observed, "It has been well said that no man ever sank under the burden of the day. It is when tomorrow's burden is added to the burden of today that the weight is more than a man can bear. Never load yourselves so, my friends. If you find yourselves so loaded, at least remember this: it is your own doing, not God's. He begs you to leave the future to Him."

Today, as a gift to yourself, to your family, and to your friends, claim the inner peace that is your spiritual birthright: the peace of

Jesus Christ. Christ is standing at the door, waiting patiently for you to invite Him to reign over your heart. His eternal peace is offered freely. Claim it today.

SOMETHING TO THINK ABOUT

Jesus offers peace that passes human understanding . . . and He wants you to make His peace your peace.

MORE IDEAS ABOUT
PEACE

The result of righteousness will be peace; the effect of righteousness will be quiet confidence forever.

Isaiah 32:17 HCSB

Peace, peace to you, and peace to him who helps you, for your God helps you.

1 Chronicles 12:18 HCSB

God has called us to peace.

1 Corinthians 7:15 NKJV

Grace, mercy, and peace will be with us from God the Father and from Jesus Christ, the Son of the Father, in truth and love.

2 John 1:3 HCSB

But now in Christ Jesus you who once were far off have been brought near by the blood of Christ. For He Himself is our peace.

Ephesians 2:13-14 NKJV

To know God as He really is—in His essential nature and character—is to arrive at a citadel of peace that circumstances may storm, but can never capture.

Catherine Marshall

That peace, which has been described and which believers enjoy, is a participation of the peace which their glorious Lord and Master himself enjoys.

Jonathan Edwards

The fruit of our placing all things in God's hands is the presence of His abiding peace in our hearts.

Hannah Whitall Smith

There may be no trumpet sound or loud applause when we make a right decision, just a calm sense of resolution and peace.

Gloria Gaither

A great many people are trying to make peace, but that has already been done. God has not left it for us to do; all we have to do is to enter into it.

D. L. Moody

Rejoicing is a matter of obedience to God—an obedience that will start you on the road to peace and contentment.

Kay Arthur

MY THOUGHTS ON . . .
Whether or not I'm really experiencing the genuine peace
that can and should be mine through Jesus.

_____

_____

_____

_____

_____

_____

A PRAYER

Dear Lord, the peace that the world offers is fleeting,
but You offer a peace that is perfect and eternal.
Let me take my concerns and burdens to You, Father,
and let me feel the spiritual abundance that You offer through
the person of Your Son, the Prince of Peace.
Amen

Lesson 21

Build a Loving Relationship with Jesus

So when they had eaten breakfast, Jesus said to Simon Peter, "Simon, son of Jonah, do you love Me more than these?" He said to Him, "Yes, Lord; You know that I love You." He said to him, "Feed My lambs." He said to him again a second time, "Simon, son of Jonah, do you love Me?" He said to Him, "Yes, Lord; You know that I love You." He said to him, "Tend My sheep." He said to him the third time, "Simon, son of Jonah, do you love Me?" Peter was grieved because He said to him the third time, "Do you love Me?" And he said to Him, "Lord, You know all things; You know that I love You." Jesus said to him, "Feed My sheep."

John 21:15-17 NKJV

THE LESSON

Three times Jesus inquired of Peter, "Do you love Me?" Thus did the Master emphasize the need for His followers to build a loving relationship with Him.

Jesus loved you so much that He endured unspeakable humiliation and suffering for you. How will you respond to Christ's sacrifice? Will you take up His cross and follow Him (Luke 9:23), or will you choose another path? When you place your hopes squarely at the foot of the cross, when you place Jesus squarely at the center of your life, you will be blessed. When you build a growing, loving relationship with the One from Galilee, your life will be changed now and forever.

The 19th-century writer Hannah Whitall Smith observed, "The crucial question for each of us is this: What do you think of Jesus, and do you yet have a personal acquaintance with Him?" Indeed, the answer to that question determines the quality, the course, and the direction of our lives today and for all eternity.

> Jesus Christ is the first and last, author and finisher, beginning and end, alpha and omega, and by Him all other things hold together.
> He must be first or nothing. God never comes next!
>
> —
>
> *Vance Havner*

The old familiar hymn begins, "What a friend we have in Jesus . . . ." No truer words were ever penned. Jesus is the sovereign Friend and ultimate Savior of mankind. Christ showed enduring love for His believers by willingly sacrificing His own life so that we might have eternal life. Now, it is our turn to become His friend.

Let us love our Savior, praise Him, and share His message of salvation with our neighbors and with the world. When we do, we demonstrate that our acquaintance with the Master is not a passing fancy; it is, instead, the cornerstone and the touchstone of our lives.

SOMETHING TO THINK ABOUT

Jesus loves you, and you, in turn, should love Him. Christ's love can—and should—be the cornerstone and the touchstone of your life.

MORE IDEAS ABOUT
LOVING JESUS

And Jesus said to them, "I am the bread of life. He who comes to Me shall never hunger, and he who believes in Me shall never thirst."

John 6:35 NKJV

Greater love has no one than this, than to lay down one's life for his friends.

John 15:13 NKJV

This is how we know that we love God's children when we love God and obey His commands.

1 John 5:2 HCSB

If you love Me, keep My commandments.

John 14:15 NKJV

You love Him, though you have not seen Him. And though not seeing Him now, you believe in Him and rejoice with inexpressible and glorious joy, because you are receiving the goal of your faith, the salvation of your souls.

1 Peter 1:8-9 HCSB

The key to my understanding of the Bible is a personal relationship to Jesus Christ.

Oswald Chambers

Jesus be mine forever, my God, my heaven, my all.

C. H. Spurgeon

Tell me the story of Jesus. Write on my heart every word. Tell me the story most precious, sweetest that ever was heard.

Fanny Crosby

I am truly happy with Jesus Christ. I couldn't live without Him. When my life gets beyond the ability to cope, He takes over.

Ruth Bell Graham

Loving Him means the thankful acceptance of all things that His love has appointed.

Elisabeth Elliot

The secret of the Christian is that he knows the absolute deity of the Lord Jesus Christ.

Oswald Chambers

MY THOUGHTS ON . . .
The sacrifice that Jesus made for me,
and the way I should respond to His sacrifice.

_____

_____

_____

_____

_____

_____

_____

_____

A PRAYER

Dear Lord, thank You for Your Son. Jesus loves me
and He shares so much with me. Let me share His love
with others so that through me, they can understand
what it means to follow Him.
Amen

Lesson 22

Give Sacrificially

*So He called His disciples to Himself and said to them,
"Assuredly, I say to you that this poor widow has put in
more than all those who have given to the treasury;
for they all put in out of their abundance, but she out of
her poverty put in all that she had, her whole livelihood."*

Mark 12:43-44 NKJV

THE LESSON

Jesus told His disciples a parable about a poor widow who gave
all she had as an offering to God. Thus Jesus encouraged His
followers to give sacrificially.

The parable about the widow who gave all she had was Jesus' way of teaching His disciples to give sacrificially. In Matthew 10:8, Christ reinforced this message: "Freely you have received, freely give" (NIV). And, of course, Christ's words still apply—as believers, we are commanded to be generous with our friends, with our families, and with those in need. We must give freely of our time, our possessions, and, most especially, our love.

> If our charities do not at all pinch or hamper us, I should say they are too small. There ought to be things we should like to do and cannot do because our charitable expenditure excludes them.
>
> —
>
> *C. S. Lewis*

Christ showed His love for us by willingly sacrificing His own life so that we might have eternal life: "But God demonstrates his own love for us in this: While we were still sinners, Christ died for us" (Romans 5:8 NIV). We, as Christ's followers, are challenged to share His love. And, when we walk each day with Jesus—and obey the commandments found in God's Holy Word—we are worthy ambassadors for Him. Just as Christ has been—and will always be—the ultimate friend to His flock, so should we be Christlike in our love and generosity to those in need. When we share the love of Christ, we share a priceless gift. As His servants, we must do no less.

So today, take God's words to heart and make this pledge: Be a cheerful, generous, courageous giver. The world needs your help, and you need the spiritual rewards that will be yours when you give it.

SOMETHING TO THINK ABOUT

God has given you countless blessings . . . and He wants you to share them.

Blessings Given | Blessings Received

MORE IDEAS ABOUT GENEROSITY

So let each one give as he purposes in his heart, not grudgingly or of necessity; for God loves a cheerful giver.

2 Corinthians 9:7 NKJV

Dear friend, you are showing your faith by whatever you do for the brothers, and this you are doing for strangers.

3 John 1:5 HCSB

In every way I've shown you that by laboring like this, it is necessary to help the weak and to keep in mind the words of the Lord Jesus, for He said, "It is more blessed to give than to receive."

Acts 20:35 HCSB

Cast your bread upon the waters, for you will find it after many days.

Ecclesiastes 11:1 NKJV

But a generous man devises generous things, and by generosity he shall stand.

Isaiah 32:8 NKJV

I can usually sense that a leading is from the Holy Spirit when it calls me to humble myself, to serve somebody, to encourage somebody, or to give something away. Very rarely will the evil one lead us to do those kind of things.

Bill Hybels

Jesus had a loving heart. If he dwells within us, hatred and bitterness will never rule us.

Billy Graham

God does not supply money to satisfy our every whim and desire. His promise is to meet our needs and provide an abundance so that we can help other people.

Larry Burkett

Let us give according to our incomes, lest God make our incomes match our gifts.

Peter Marshall

For many of us, the great obstacle to charity lies not in our luxurious living or desire for more money, but in our fear of insecurity.

C. S. Lewis

All kindness and good deeds, we must keep silent. The result will be an inner reservoir of power.

Catherine Marshall

MY THOUGHTS ON . . .

Ways that I can be more generous today.

By giving of my time

A PRAYER

Lord, make me a generous and cheerful giver.
Help me to give generously of my time and my possessions
as I care for those in need. And, make me a humble giver,
Lord, so that all the glory and the praise might be Yours.

Amen

Lesson 23

Let Your Light Shine Brightly

Then Jesus spoke to them again: "I am the light of the world. Anyone who follows Me will never walk in the darkness, but will have the light of life."

John 8:12 HCSB

THE LESSON

Jesus instructed His followers to walk in the light and, by doing so, become powerful examples to the world. And the same instructions apply to us: we must walk—and live—in the light, not the darkness.

Whether we like it or not, all of us are role models. Our friends and family members watch our actions and, as followers of Christ, we are obliged to act accordingly.

What kind of example are you? Are you the kind of person whose life serves as a genuine example of righteousness? Does your behavior serve as a positive role model for others? Are you the kind of believer whose actions, day in and day out, are based upon kindness, faithfulness, and a love for the Lord? If so, you are not only blessed by God, but you are also a powerful force for good in a world that desperately needs positive influences such as yours.

Phillips Brooks had simple advice for believers of every generation; he said, "Be such a person, and live such a life, that if every person were such as you, and every life a life like yours, this earth would be God's Paradise." And that's precisely the kind of Christian you should strive to be . . . but it isn't always easy.

> A holy life will produce the deepest impression. Lighthouses blow no horns; they only shine.
>
> —
>
> *D. L. Moody*

You live in a dangerous, temptation-filled world. That's why you encounter so many opportunities to stray from God's commandments. Resist those temptations! When you do, you'll earn God's blessings, and you'll serve as a positive role model for your family and friends.

Corrie ten Boom advised, "Don't worry about what you do not understand. Worry about what you do understand in the Bible but do not live by." And that's sound advice because your families and friends are watching . . . and so, for that matter, is God.

SOMETHING TO THINK ABOUT

God wants you to be a good example to your family, to your friends, and to the world.

MORE IDEAS ABOUT
EXAMPLE

You should be an example to the believers in speech, in conduct, in love, in faith, in purity.

1 Timothy 4:12 HCSB

Do everything without grumbling and arguing, so that you may be blameless and pure.

Philippians 2:14–15 HCSB

Set an example of good works yourself, with integrity and dignity in your teaching.

Titus 2:7 HCSB

For the kingdom of God is not in word but in power.

1 Corinthians 4:20 NKJV

For this is the will of God, that by doing good you may put to silence the ignorance of foolish men as free, yet not using liberty as a cloak for vice, but as bondservants of God.

1 Peter 2:15-16 NKJV

Integrity of heart is indispensable.

John Calvin

If I take care of my character, my reputation will take care of itself.

D. L. Moody

There is no way to grow a saint overnight. Character, like the oak tree, does not spring up like a mushroom.

Vance Havner

Your light is the truth of the Gospel message itself as well as your witness as to Who Jesus is and what He has done for you. Don't hide it.

Anne Graham Lotz

You can never separate a leader's actions from his character.

John Maxwell

There is nothing anybody else can do that can stop God from using us . . . . We can turn everything into a testimony.

Corrie ten Boom

MY THOUGHTS ON . . .

The steps I should take to be a better example to
my family members, to my friends, and to my coworkers.

_____

_____

_____

_____

_____

_____

_____

A PRAYER

Dear Lord, help me be a worthy example to my friends
and to my family. Let the things that I say and the things
that I do show everyone what it means to be
a follower of Your Son.
Amen

Lesson 24

Be Humble

Let this mind be in you which was also in Christ Jesus,
who, being in the form of God, did not consider it robbery
to be equal with God, but made Himself of no reputation,
taking the form of a bondservant, and coming in
the likeness of men. And being found in appearance
as a man, He humbled Himself and became obedient to
the point of death, even the death of the cross.

Philippians 2:5-8 NKJV

THE LESSON

Jesus showed humility when He came from heaven and took
on the role of servant. And as we consider Christ's sacrifice,
we, too, must be humble.

Are you a humble believer who always gives credit where credit is due? If so, you are both wise and blessed.

Dietrich Bonhoeffer observed, "It is very easy to overestimate the importance of our own achievements in comparison with what we owe others." How true. Even those of us who consider ourselves "self-made" men and women are deeply indebted to more people than we can count. Our first and greatest indebtedness, of course, is to God and His only begotten Son. But we are also indebted to ancestors, parents, teachers, friends, spouses, family members, coworkers, fellow believers . . . and the list goes on.

> Because Christ Jesus came to the world clothed in humility, he will always be found among those who are clothed with humility. He will be found among the humble people.
>
> —
>
> A. W. Tozer

With so many people who rightfully deserve to share the credit for our successes, how can we gloat? The answer, of course, is that we should not. But we inhabit a world in which far too many of our role models are remarkably haughty and surprisingly self-centered (hopefully, these are not your role models).

The Bible contains stern warnings against the sin of pride. One such warning is found in Proverbs 16:8: "Pride goes before destruction, and a haughty spirit before a fall" (NKJV). God's Word makes it clear: Pride and destruction are traveling companions (but hopefully, they're not your traveling companions).

150

Jonathan Edwards observed, "Nothing sets a person so much out of the devil's reach as humility." So, if you're celebrating a worthwhile accomplishment, don't invite the devil to celebrate with you. Instead of puffing out your chest and saying, "Look at me!" give credit where credit is due, starting with God. And rest assured: There is no such thing as a self-made man or woman. All of us are made by God . . . and He deserves the glory, not us.

SOMETHING TO THINK ABOUT

God favors the humble just as surely as He disciplines the proud. You must remain humble or face the consequences.

More Ideas about Humility

If My people who are called by My name will humble themselves, and pray and seek My face, and turn from their wicked ways, then I will hear from heaven, and will forgive their sin and heal their land.

2 Chronicles 7:14 NKJV

Likewise, you younger men, be subject to the elders.

1 Peter 5:5 HCSB

Therefore, God's chosen ones, holy and loved, put on heartfelt compassion, kindness, humility, gentleness, and patience.

Colossians 3:12 HCSB

Humble yourselves before the Lord, and He will exalt you.

James 4:10 HCSB

For everyone who exalts himself will be humbled, and the one who humbles himself will be exalted.

Luke 14:11 HCSB

Jesus had a humble heart. If He abides in us, pride will never dominate our lives.

Billy Graham

Humility is the fairest and rarest flower that blooms.

Charles Swindoll

That's what I love about serving God. In His eyes, there are no little people . . . because there are no big people. We are all on the same playing field. We all start at square one. No one has it better than the other, or possesses unfair advantage.

Joni Eareckson Tada

All kindness and good deeds, we must keep silent. The result will be an inner reservoir of personality power.

Catherine Marshall

Let the love of Christ be believed in and felt in your hearts, and it will humble you.

C. H. Spurgeon

God gives grace to the humble, not to the prideful. If we assume self-advancing attitudes, we've missed His gift of favor.

Franklin Graham

MY THOUGHTS ON . . .

The need to be humble, and the need to focus on God's blessings.

_____

_____

_____

_____

_____

_____

_____

A PRAYER

Dear Lord, keep me humble. It is the nature of mankind
to be prideful, and I am no exception. When I am boastful,
keep me mindful that all my gifts come from You. Let me grow
beyond my need for earthly praise, Father, and let me look
only to You for approval. You are the Giver of all things good;
let me give all the glory to You.

Amen

Lesson 25

When Confronting Evil, Don't Be Neutral

*Then Jesus went into the temple of God and drove out
all those who bought and sold in the temple,
and overturned the tables of the money changers
and the seats of those who sold doves.*

Matthew 21:12 NKJV

THE LESSON

God's Word condemns random anger, but Jesus demonstrates
that anger directed toward evil is justified.

Unbridled anger is counterproductive, and the Bible is filled with messages that warn us to control our tempers. But sometimes, anger can be a good thing.

In the 21st chapter of Matthew, we are told how Christ responded when He confronted the evildoings of those who invaded His Father's house of worship. Jesus physically removed the profiteers from the temple. By doing so, He proved that righteous indignation is an appropriate response to evil.

We live in a society that encourages us to "look the other way" when we are confronted with evildoings. The world encourages us to view morality as a relative phenomenon, something that changes with societal trends. When we observe wrongdoing, we are encouraged to "live and let live." But God intends that we stand up for our beliefs, and He intends that we stand up for Him.

> Unrighteous anger feeds the ego and produces the poison of selfishness in the heart.
>
> —
>
> *Warren Wiersbe*

If you wish to build a life that is pleasing to your Creator, you should stand up to the temptations and distractions of modern-day society. Standing up for yourself—and for God—isn't always easy when so many societal forces are struggling to compromise your character . . . but with God's help, you can do it.

So, when you come face to face with the devil's handiwork, don't be satisfied to remain safely on the sidelines. Instead, follow in the footsteps of your Savior. Jesus never compromised with evil, and neither should you.

SOMETHING TO THINK ABOUT

Because God is just, He rewards good behavior just as surely as He punishes sin. And there are no loopholes.

MORE IDEAS ABOUT
RIGHTEOUSNESS

For the eyes of the Lord are on the righteous, and His ears are open to their prayers; but the face of the Lord is against those who do evil.

1 Peter 3:12 NKJV

And you shall do what is right and good in the sight of the Lord, that it may be well with you.

Deuteronomy 6:18 NKJV

Test all things; hold fast what is good. Abstain from every form of evil.

1 Thessalonians 5:21-22 NKJV

Flee from youthful passions, and pursue righteousness, faith, love, and peace, along with those who call on the Lord from a pure heart.

2 Timothy 2:22 HCSB

And the fruit of righteousness is sown in peace by those who make peace.

James 3:18 HCSB

The greatest enemy of holiness is not passion; it is apathy.

John Eldredge

You have to say "yes" to God first before you can effectively say "no" to the devil.

Vance Havner

The first step on the way to victory is to recognize the enemy.

Corrie ten Boom

Christianity isn't a religion about going to Sunday school, potluck suppers, being nice, holding car washes, sending your secondhand clothes off to Mexico—as good as those things might be. This is a world at war.

John Eldredge

Sin must be destroyed, not corrected.

Oswald Chambers

Give Satan an inch and he'll be a ruler.

Anonymous

MY THOUGHTS ON . . .
My need to stand up for my beliefs,
even when it's difficult or unpopular to do so.

A PRAYER

Lord, give me the wisdom to know when anger is appropriate.
Give me the courage to fight injustice, the wisdom
to avoid temptation, and the perseverance to follow
in the footsteps of Your Son every day of my life.
Amen

Lesson 26

Don't Be Too Quick to Judge Others

When Jesus stood up, He said to her, "Woman, where are they? Has no one condemned you?" "No one, Lord," she answered. "Neither do I condemn you," said Jesus. "Go, and from now on do not sin any more."

John 8:10–11 HCSB

THE LESSON

Jesus challenged the religious leaders of the day to cast stones only if they had never committed a sin. Then, He told the woman who had been caught in adultery to go and sin no more.

Even the most devoted Christians may fall prey to a powerful yet subtle temptation: the temptation to judge others. But as believers, we are commanded to refrain from such behavior. The warning of Matthew 7:1 is clear: "Judge not, that ye be not judged" (KJV).

Are you one of those people who finds it easy to judge others? If so, it's time to make radical changes in the way you view the world and the people who inhabit it.

When considering the shortcomings of others, you must remember this: in matters of judgment, God does not need (or want) your help. Why? Because God is perfectly capable of judging the human heart . . . while you are not. This message is made clear by the teachings of Jesus.

> Give me such love for God and men as will blot out all hatred and bitterness.
>
> —
>
> *Dietrich Bonhoeffer*

As Jesus came upon a young woman who had been condemned by the Pharisees, He spoke not only to the crowd that was gathered there, but also to all generations, when He warned, "He that is without sin among you, let him first cast a stone at her" (John 8:7 KJV). Christ's message is clear: because we are all sinners, we are commanded to refrain from judging others. Yet the irony is this: It is precisely because we are sinners that we are so quick to judge.

All of us have all fallen short of God's laws, and none of us, therefore, are qualified to "cast the first stone." Thankfully, God has forgiven us, and we, too, must forgive others. Let us refrain, then, from judging our family members, our friends, and our loved ones. Instead, let us forgive them and love them in the same way that God has forgiven us.

SOMETHING TO THINK ABOUT

To the extent you judge others, so, too, will you be judged. So you must, to the best of your ability, refrain from judgmental thoughts and words.

MORE IDEAS ABOUT
JUDGING OTHERS

Therefore, anyone of you who judges is without excuse. For when you judge another, you condemn yourself, since you, the judge, do the same things.

Romans 2:1 HCSB

Speak and act as those who will be judged by the law of freedom. For judgment is without mercy to the one who hasn't shown mercy. Mercy triumphs over judgment.

James 2:12-13 HCSB

"Why do you look at the speck in your brother's eye, but don't notice the log in your own eye? Or how can you say to your brother, 'Let me take the speck out of your eye,' and look, there's a log in your eye? Hypocrite! First take the log out of your eye, and then you will see clearly to take the speck out of your brother's eye."

Matthew 7:3-5 HCSB

Do not judge, and you will not be judged. Do not condemn, and you will not be condemned. Forgive, and you will be forgiven.

Luke 6:37 HCSB

Christians think they are prosecuting attorneys or judges, when, in reality, God has called all of us to be witnesses.

Warren Wiersbe

Judging draws the judgment of others.

Catherine Marshall

Being critical of others, including God, is one way we try to avoid facing and judging our own sins.

Warren Wiersbe

Our Lord worked with people as they were, and He was patient—not tolerant of sin, but compassionate.

Vance Havner

Don't judge other people more harshly than you want God to judge you.

Marie T. Freeman

An individual Christian may see fit to give up all sorts of things for special reasons—marriage, or meat, or beer, or cinema; but the moment he starts saying these things are bad in themselves, or looking down his nose at other people who do use them, he has taken the wrong turn.

C. S. Lewis

MY THOUGHTS ON . . .
The people whom I am tempted to judge . . .
and what God's Word teaches me about judging others.

_____

_____

_____

_____

_____

_____

_____

A PRAYER

Lord, it's so easy to judge other people, but it's also easy to
misjudge them. Only You can judge a human heart, Lord,
so let me love my friends and neighbors, and let me help them,
but never let me judge them.
Amen

Lesson 27

Pray More

Very early in the morning, while it was still dark,
He got up, went out, and made His way to
a deserted place. And He was praying there.
Mark 1:35 HCSB

THE LESSON

Jesus prayed early and often. He engaged in a constant
conversation with His Father . . . and we should do likewise.

Does prayer play an important role in your life? Is prayer an integral part of your daily routine, or is it a hit-or-miss activity? Do you "pray without ceasing," or is your prayer life an afterthought? If you genuinely wish to receive that abundance that Christ promises in John 10:10, then you must pray constantly . . . and you must never underestimate the power of prayer.

As you contemplate the quality of your prayer life, here are a few things to consider: 1. God hears our prayers and answers them (Jeremiah 29:11-12). 2. God promises that the prayers of righteous men and women can accomplish great things (James 5:16). 3. God invites us to be still and to feel His presence (Psalm 46:10).

> Be careful what you pray for—because everything and anything is possible through the power of prayer!
>
> —
>
> *Barbara Johnson*

So pray. Start praying in the early morning and keep praying until you fall off to sleep at night. Pray about matters great and small; and be watchful for the answers that God most assuredly sends your way.

Daily prayer and meditation is a matter of will and habit. When you organize your day to include quiet moments with God, you'll soon discover that no time is more precious than the silent moments you spend with Him.

The quality of your spiritual life will be in direct proportion to the quality of your prayer life. So do yourself a favor: instead of turning things over in your mind, turn them over to God in prayer. Instead of worrying about your next decision, ask God to lead the way. Don't limit your prayers to meals or to bedtime. Pray constantly because God is listening—and He wants to hear from you. And without question, you need to hear from Him.

SOMETHING TO THINK ABOUT

Prayer changes things—and it changes you—so pray.

MORE IDEAS ABOUT
PRAYER

Rejoice always! Pray constantly. Give thanks in everything, for this is God's will for you in Christ Jesus.

1 Thessalonians 5:16-18 HCSB

Therefore I say to you, whatever things you ask when you pray, believe that you receive them, and you will have them.

Mark 11:24 NKJV

Therefore I want the men in every place to pray, lifting up holy hands without anger or argument.

1 Timothy 2:8 HCSB

Is anyone among you suffering? He should pray. Is anyone cheerful? He should sing praises.

James 5:13 HCSB

Watch therefore, and pray always that you may be counted worthy to escape all these things that will come to pass, and to stand before the Son of Man.

Luke 21:36 NKJV

When there is a matter that requires definite prayer, pray until you believe God and until you can thank Him for His answer.

Hannah Whitall Smith

I live in the spirit of prayer; I pray as I walk, when I lie down, and when I rise. And, the answers are always coming.

George Mueller

When you ask God to do something, don't ask timidly; put your whole heart into it.

Marie T. Freeman

As we join together in prayer, we draw on God's enabling might in a way that multiplies our own efforts many times over.

Shirley Dobson

The center of power is not to be found in summit meetings or in peace conferences. It is not in Peking or Washington or the United Nations, but rather where a child of God prays in the power of the Spirit for God's will to be done in her life, in her home, and in the world around her.

Ruth Bell Graham

Prayer is an expression of a clear, simple relationship with God.

Henry Blackaby

MY THOUGHTS ON . . .
The role that prayer currently plays in my life,
and the role that it should play.

_____

_____

_____

_____

_____

_____

_____

A PRAYER

Dear Lord, Your Holy Word commands me to pray without
ceasing. Let me take everything to You in prayer.
When I am discouraged, let me pray. When I am lonely,
let me take my sorrows to You. When I grieve, let me take
my tears to You, Father, in prayer. And when I am joyful,
let me offer up prayers of thanksgiving. In all things great
and small, at all times, whether happy or sad, let me seek
Your wisdom and Your grace . . . in prayer.
Amen

PRAY31

One Million, One Month, One Nation
October 2014

This year, do the most important thing your church can do for America...
PRAY

During the month of October...
thousands of churches will be praying for our country. Through an historic initiative called **Pray31**, congregations from coast to coast will experience the power of intensive, purposeful prayer. It's part of a nationwide movement with the ultimate goal of *one million people praying for one month for this one nation under God.*

For more information contact Karen Dyer: 574-291-5704 church office or 291-7722 home.

To join the *Pray31* team write your name below, tear off and place in the offering or return to the church office.

Yes, I want to join the Pray31 team.

_____

Experiencing the Journey of PRAY31 at South Side Church of God

One Million, One Month, One Nation
October 2014

A Simple Plan, A unique resource

Pray31 is based on a simple plan: ***31 days of focused prayer for America***. The guide for this 31-day journey is a unique resource, the ***Pray31 U.S. Prayer Atlas***. Church members use the Atlas for just a few minutes every day, praying for that day's requests. By the end of the 31 days, they will have prayed across America. In the process, their own lives will be spiritually enriched and energized.

Pray31 will not interfere with other church activities. In fact, it enhances all other activities as it deepens the devotional life of the church.

Pray with love.
Hope to have faith
Prayers are for Christ

Lesson 28

Share God's Good News

Then He said to them, "Go into all the world and preach the gospel to the whole creation."

Mark 16:15 HCSB

THE LESSON

Jesus clearly instructs us to go out into the world and share His Good News. Each of us can be a spokesperson for Christ—and that's precisely what each of us must do.

Are you a bashful Christian, one who is afraid to speak up for your Savior? Do you allow others to share their testimonies while you stand on the sidelines, reluctant to share yours? After His resurrection, Jesus addressed His disciples:

"But the eleven disciples proceeded to Galilee, to the mountain which Jesus had designated. When they saw Him, they worshiped Him; but some were doubtful. And Jesus came up and spoke to them, saying, 'All authority has been given to Me in heaven and on earth. Go therefore and make disciples of all the nations, baptizing them in the name of the Father and the Son and the Holy Spirit, teaching them to observe all that I commanded you; and lo, I am with you always, even to the end of the age'" (Matthew 28:16–20 NASB).

> You can go to the mission field in person, by prayer, by provision, or by proxy. But remember, there is a mission field across the street as well as across the sea.
>
> —
>
> *Vance Havner*

Christ's great commission applies to Christians of every generation, including our own. As believers, we are called to share the Good News of Jesus Christ with our families, with our neighbors, and with the world. Yet many of us are slow to obey the last commandment of the risen Christ; we simply don't do our best to "make disciples of all the nations." Although our personal testimonies are vitally important, we sometimes hesitate to share our experiences. And that's unfortunate.

Billy Graham observed, "Our faith grows by expression. If we want to keep our faith, we must share it." If you are a follower of Christ, the time to express your belief in Him is now.

You know how Jesus has touched your heart; help Him do the same for others. You must do likewise, and you must do so today. Tomorrow may indeed be too late.

SOMETHING TO THINK ABOUT

God's Word clearly instructs you to share His Good News with the world. If you're willing, God will empower you to share your faith.

More Ideas about
Missions

After this the Lord appointed 70 others, and He sent them ahead of Him in pairs to every town and place where He Himself was about to go. He told them: "The harvest is abundant, but the workers are few. Therefore, pray to the Lord of the harvest to send out workers into His harvest. Now go; I'm sending you out like lambs among wolves."

Luke 10:1-3 HCSB

And I say to you, anyone who acknowledges Me before men, the Son of Man will also acknowledge him before the angels of God; but whoever denies Me before men will be denied before the angels of God.

Luke 12:8-9 HCSB

The following night, the Lord stood by him and said, "Have courage! For as you have testified about Me in Jerusalem, so you must also testify in Rome."

Acts 23:11 HCSB

I will also make you a light for the nations, to be My salvation to the ends of the earth.

Isaiah 49:6 HCSB

What I tell you in the dark, speak in the light. What you hear in a whisper, proclaim on the housetops.

Matthew 10:27 HCSB

The evangelistic harvest is always urgent. The destiny of men and of nations is always being decided. Every generation is strategic. We are not responsible for the past generation, and we cannot bear the full responsibility for the next one, but we do have our generation. God will hold us responsible as to how well we fulfill our responsibilities to this age and take advantage of our opportunities.

Billy Graham

Our commission is quite specific. We are told to be His witness to all nations. For us, as His disciples, to refuse any part of this commission frustrates the love of Jesus Christ, the Son of God.

Catherine Marshall

We are now, a very, very few feeble workers, scattering the grain broadcast according as time and strength permit. God will give the harvest; doubt it not. But the laborers are few.

Lottie Moon

God is not saving the world; it is done. Our business is to get men and women to realize it.

Oswald Chambers

Missions is God finding those whose hearts are right with Him and placing them where they can make a difference for His kingdom.

Henry Blackaby

MY THOUGHTS ON . . .
Ways that I can be a better witness for Christ at home
and around the world.

_____

_____

_____

_____

_____

_____

_____

A PRAYER

Lord, even if I never leave home, make me a missionary
for You. Let me share the Good News of Your Son,
and let me tell of Your love and of Your grace.
Make me a faithful servant for You, Father, now and forever.
Amen

Lesson 29

Don't Worry

But seek first the kingdom of God and His righteousness,
and all these things shall be added to you.
Therefore do not worry about tomorrow,
for tomorrow will worry about its own things.
Sufficient for the day is its own trouble.

Matthew 6:33-34 NKJV

THE LESSON

As citizens of our modern, market-driven world, we're tempted to worry about food, fashion, fads, and almost everything else, for that matter. But if we're wise, we learn to worry less by seeking God's kingdom first. When we do, everything else falls into place.

Have you acquired the habit of worrying about almost everything under the sun? If so, it's a habit you should break.

Even if you're a very faithful Christian, you may be plagued by occasional periods of discouragement and doubt. Even though you trust God's promise of salvation—even though you sincerely believe in God's love and protection—you may find yourself upset by the countless details of everyday life. Jesus understood your concerns when He spoke the reassuring words found in the 6th chapter of Matthew:

"Therefore I say to you, do not worry about your life, what you will eat or what you will drink; nor about your body, what you will put on. Is not life more than food and the body more than clothing? Look at the birds of the air, for they neither sow nor reap nor gather into barns; yet your heavenly Father feeds them. Are you not of more value than they?" (vv. 25-27 NKJV)

> Pray,
> and let God worry.
>
> —
>
> *Martin Luther*

Where is the best place to take your worries? Take them to God. Take your troubles to Him; take your fears to Him; take your doubts to Him; take your weaknesses to Him; take your sorrows to Him . . . and leave them all there. Seek protection from the One who offers you eternal salvation; build your spiritual house upon the Rock that cannot be moved.

Perhaps you are concerned about your future, your relationships, or your finances. Or perhaps you are simply a "worrier" by nature. If so, choose to make Matthew 6 a regular part of your daily Bible reading. This beautiful passage will remind you that God still sits in His heaven and you are His beloved child. Then, perhaps, you will worry a little less and trust God a little more, and that's as it should be because God is trustworthy . . . and you are protected.

SOMETHING TO THINK ABOUT

You have worries, but God has solutions. Your challenge is to trust Him to solve the problems that you can't.

MORE IDEAS ABOUT
WORRY

Don't worry about anything, but in everything, through prayer and petition with thanksgiving, let your requests be made known to God.

Philippians 4:6 HCSB

Your heart must not be troubled. Believe in God; believe also in Me.

John 14:1 HCSB

Now it happened as they went that He entered a certain village; and a certain woman named Martha welcomed Him into her house. And she had a sister called Mary, who also sat at Jesus' feet and heard His word. But Martha was distracted with much serving, and she approached Him and said, "Lord, do You not care that my sister has left me to serve alone? Therefore tell her to help me." And Jesus answered and said to her, "Martha, Martha, you are worried and troubled about many things. But one thing is needed, and Mary has chosen that good part, which will not be taken away from her."

Luke 10:38-42 NKJV

Don't worry about your life, what you will eat or what you will drink; or about your body, what you will wear. Isn't life more than food and the body more than clothing?

Matthew 6:25 HCSB

Worry is the senseless process of cluttering up tomorrow's opportunities with leftover problems from today.

Barbara Johnson

Never yield to gloomy anticipation. Place your hope and confidence in God. He has no record of failure.

Mrs. Charles E. Cowman

Today is mine. Tomorrow is none of my business. If I peer anxiously into the fog of the future, I will strain my spiritual eyes so that I will not see clearly what is required of me now.

Elisabeth Elliott

Worry and anxiety are sand in the machinery of life; faith is the oil.

E. Stanley Jones

Earthly fears are no fears at all. Answer the big question of eternity, and the little questions of life fall into perspective.

Max Lucado

MY THOUGHTS ON . . .
The things that I worry about, and the strength that I can, and should, draw from God's promises.

_____

_____

_____

_____

_____

_____

_____

A PRAYER

Dear Lord, wherever I find myself, let me celebrate more and worry less. When my faith begins to waver, help me to trust You more. Then, with praise on my lips and the love of Your Son in my heart, let me live courageously, faithfully, prayerfully, and thankfully this day and every day.

Amen

Lesson 30

You Have a Place in Heaven

*In My Father's house are many dwelling places; if not,
I would have told you. I am going away to prepare
a place for you. If I go away and prepare a place for you,
I will come back and receive you to Myself,
so that where I am you may be also.*

John 14:2-3 HCSB

THE LESSON

Jesus promises that He has gone to prepare an eternal resting place, and He promises that He will return and carry His children home.

Sometimes life's inevitable troubles and heartbreaks are easier to tolerate when we remind ourselves that heaven is our true home. An old hymn contains the words, "This world is not my home; I'm just passing through." Thank goodness!

For believers, death is not an ending; it is a beginning. For believers, the grave is not a final resting-place; it is a place of transition. Death can never claim those who have accepted Christ as their personal Savior. Christ has promised that He has gone to prepare a glorious home in heaven—a timeless, blessed gift to His children—and Jesus always keeps His promises.

> No reunion in history can even foreshadow what joy we will experience as we see loved ones and friends who went on before us.
> We are known.
> We are recognized.
>
> —
>
> *Bill Bright*

If you've committed your life to Christ, your time here on earth is merely a preparation for a far different life to come: your eternal life with Jesus and a host of fellow believers.

So, while this world can be a place of temporary hardship and temporary suffering, you can be comforted in the knowledge that God offers you a permanent home that is free from all suffering and pain. Please take God at His word. When you do, you we can withstand any problem, knowing that your troubles are temporary, but that heaven is not.

SOMETHING TO THINK ABOUT

God has created heaven and given you a way to get there. The rest is up to you.

More Ideas about
Heaven

Be glad and rejoice, because your reward is great in heaven.

Matthew 5:12 HCSB

He also raised us up with Him and seated us with Him in the heavens, in Christ Jesus, so that in the coming ages He might display the immeasurable riches of His grace in His kindness to us in Christ Jesus.

Ephesians 2:6-7 HCSB

Our citizenship is in heaven, from which we also eagerly wait for a Savior, the Lord Jesus Christ.

Philippians 3:20 HCSB

As you go, announce this: "The kingdom of heaven has come near."

Matthew 10:7 HCSB

One of these days, our Father will scoop us up in His strong arms and we will hear Him say those sweet and comforting words, "Come on, child. We're going home."

Gloria Gaither

Considering how I prepare for my children when I know they are coming home, I love to think of the preparations God is making for my homecoming one day. He knows the colors I love, the scenery I enjoy, the things that make me happy, all the personal details.

Anne Graham Lotz

The believing Christian has hope as he stands at the grave of a loved one who is with the Lord, for he knows that the separation is not forever. It is a glorious truth that those who are in Christ never see each other for the last time.

Billy Graham

What joy that the Bible tells us the great comfort that the best is yet to be. Our outlook goes beyond this world.

Corrie ten Boom

Heaven itself will reflect the character of our great God. It will be a place of holiness, righteousness, love, justice, mercy, peace, order, and His sovereign rule.

Bill Bright

MY THOUGHTS ON . . .
My need to praise God for the gift of eternal life.

_____

_____

_____

_____

_____

_____

_____

A PRAYER

Dear Lord, I thank You for the gift of eternal life
that is mine through Your Son Jesus. I will keep the promise
of heaven in my heart today and every day.
Amen

More from
God's Word

Abundance

And God is able to make every grace overflow to you, so that in every way, always having everything you need, you may excel in every good work.

2 Corinthians 9:8 HCSB

Until now you have asked for nothing in My name. Ask and you will receive, that your joy may be complete.

John 16:24 HCSB

Come to terms with God and be at peace; in this way good will come to you.

Job 22:21 HCSB

My cup runs over. Surely goodness and mercy shall follow me all the days of my life; and I will dwell in the house of the Lord forever.

Psalm 23:5-6 NKJV

And He said to them, "Take heed and beware of covetousness, for one's life does not consist in the abundance of the things he possesses."

Luke 12:15 NKJV

I have come that they may have life, and that they may have it more abundantly.

—

John 10:10 NKJV

Accepting Christ

For God loved the world in this way: He gave His only Son, so that everyone who believes in Him will not perish but have eternal life.

John 3:16 HCSB

Yet we know that no one is justified by the works of the law but by faith in Jesus Christ. And we have believed in Christ Jesus, so that we might be justified by faith in Christ and not by the works of the law, because by the works of the law no human being will be justified.

Galatians 2:16 HCSB

Whoever believes that Jesus is the Christ is born of God, and everyone who loves Him who begot also loves him who is begotten of Him.

1 John 5:1 NKJV

God wanted to make known to those among the Gentiles the glorious wealth of this mystery, which is Christ in you, the hope of glory.

Colossians 1:27 HCSB

And we have seen and testify
that the Father has sent the Son
as Savior of the world.

—

1 John 4:14 NKJV

Christ's Sacrifice

For Christ also died for sins once for all, the just for the unjust, so that He might bring us to God, having been put to death in the flesh, but made alive in the spirit.

1 Peter 3:18 NASB

Everyone has to die once, then face the consequences. Christ's death was also a one-time event, but it was a sacrifice that took care of sins forever. And so, when he next appears, the outcome for those eager to greet him is, precisely, salvation.

Hebrews 9:27-28 MSG

For when we were still without strength, in due time Christ died for the ungodly.

Romans 5:6 NKJV

But God demonstrates His own love toward us, in that while we were still sinners, Christ died for us.

Romans 5:8 NKJV

Blessings

You will show me the path of life; in Your presence is fullness of joy; at Your right hand are pleasures forevermore.

Psalm 16:11 NKJV

I will make them and the area around My hill a blessing: I will send down showers in their season—showers of blessing.

Ezekiel 34:26 HCSB

Obey My voice, and I will be your God, and you shall be my people. And walk in all the ways that I have commanded you, that it may be well with you.

Jeremiah 7:23 NKJV

The Lord bless you and keep you; the Lord make His face shine upon you, and be gracious to you.

Numbers 6:24-25 NKJV

Blessed is a man who endures trials, because when he passes the test he will receive the crown of life that He has promised to those who love Him.

James 1:12 HCSB

Adversity

When you are in distress and all these things have happened to you, you will return to the Lord your God in later days and obey Him. He will not leave you, destroy you, or forget the covenant with your fathers that He swore to them by oath, because the Lord your God is a compassionate God.

Deuteronomy 4:30-31 HCSB

Whatever has been born of God conquers the world. This is the victory that has conquered the world: our faith.

1 John 5:4 HCSB

Dear friends, when the fiery ordeal arises among you to test you, don't be surprised by it, as if something unusual were happening to you. Instead, as you share in the sufferings of the Messiah rejoice, so that you may also rejoice with great joy at the revelation of His glory.

1 Peter 4:12-13 HCSB

We are pressured in every way but not crushed; we are perplexed but not in despair.

2 Corinthians 4:8 HCSB

*I called to the Lord in my distress;
I called to my God.
From His temple He heard my voice.*

—

2 Samuel 22:7 HCSB

Evil

Therefore, submit to God. But resist the Devil, and he will flee from you. Draw near to God, and He will draw near to you. Cleanse your hands, sinners, and purify your hearts, double-minded people!

James 4:7-8 HCSB

Do not be conquered by evil, but conquer evil with good.

Romans 12:21 HCSB

For everyone who practices wicked things hates the light and avoids it, so that his deeds may not be exposed. But anyone who lives by the truth comes to the light, so that his works may be shown to be accomplished by God.

John 3:20–21 HCSB

He replied, "Every plant that My heavenly Father didn't plant will be uprooted."

Matthew 15:13 HCSB

But the path of the just is like the shining sun, that shines ever brighter unto the perfect day. The way of the wicked is like darkness; they do not know what makes them stumble.

Proverbs 4:18-19 NKJV

Don't consider yourself to be wise;
fear the Lord
and turn away from evil.

—

Proverbs 3:7 HCSB

Fearing God

Don't consider yourself to be wise; fear the Lord and turn away from evil.

Proverbs 3:7 HCSB

The fear of the Lord is the beginning of knowledge, but fools despise wisdom and instruction.

Proverbs 1:7 NKJV

The fear of the Lord is the beginning of wisdom, and the knowledge of the Holy One is understanding.

Proverbs 9:10 HCSB

The fear of the Lord is the beginning of wisdom; all who follow His instructions have good insight.

Psalm 111:10 HCSB

The fear of the Lord is a fountain of life, turning people from the snares of death.

Proverbs 14:27 HCSB

To fear the Lord is to hate evil.

—

Proverbs 8:13 HCSB

God's Presence

Draw near to God, and He will draw near to you.

James 4:8 HCSB

You will seek Me and find Me when you search for Me with all your heart.

Jeremiah 29:13 HCSB

The Lord is near all who call out to Him, all who call out to Him with integrity. He fulfills the desires of those who fear Him; He hears their cry for help and saves them.

Psalm 145:18-19 HCSB

Surely goodness and mercy shall follow me all the days of my life: and I will dwell in the house of the Lord for ever.

Psalm 23:6 KJV

I am not alone, because the Father is with Me.

John 16:32 HCSB

Putting God First

You shall have no other gods before Me.

Exodus 20:3 NKJV

Be careful not to forget the Lord.

Deuteronomy 6:12 HCSB

It is good to give thanks to the Lord, and to sing praises to Your name, O Most High; to declare Your lovingkindness in the morning, and Your faithfulness every night.

Psalm 92:1-2 NKJV

Love the Lord your God with all your heart, with all your soul, and with all your strength.

Deuteronomy 6:5 HCSB

The Devil said to Him, "I will give You their splendor and all this authority, because it has been given over to me, and I can give it to anyone I want. If You, then, will worship me, all will be Yours." And Jesus answered him, "It is written: You shall worship the Lord your God, and Him alone you shall serve."

Luke 4:6-8 HCSB

Happiness

How happy are those whose way is blameless, who live according to the law of the Lord! Happy are those who keep His decrees and seek Him with all their heart.

Psalm 119:1-2 HCSB

If they serve Him obediently, they will end their days in prosperity and their years in happiness.

Job 36:11 HCSB

The one who understands a matter finds success, and the one who trusts in the Lord will be happy.

Proverbs 16:20 HCSB

Happy are the people whose strength is in You, whose hearts are set on pilgrimage.

Psalm 84:5 HCSB

How happy is the man who does not follow the advice of the wicked, or take the path of sinners, or join a group of mockers!

Psalm 1:1 HCSB

*A joyful heart is good medicine,
but a broken spirit
dries up the bones.*

—

Proverbs 17:22 HCSB

Then Jesus spoke to them again:
"I am the light of the world.
Anyone who follows Me will never
walk in the darkness,
but will have the light of life."

—

John 8:12 HCSB